GREECE

MEDITERRANEAN CUISINE

GREECE

MEDITERRANEAN CUISINE

KÖNEMANN

Contents

List of Recipes

Difficulty:

☆	Easy
☆☆	Medium
☆☆☆	Difficult

Hot & Cold Appetizers 8

Soups 38

Vegetable Dishes 62

Fish & Seafood 82

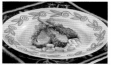

Meat & Poultry 114

Desserts & Pastries 158

Hot & Cold Appetizers

Smoked Eggplant with a

Preparation time: 45 minutes
Cooking time: 40 minutes
Difficulty: ★

Serves 4

4	eggplants
1	lemon
½	onion
2 cloves	garlic
1 sprig	thyme (optional)
3 tbsp	olive oil
2 tbsp	red wine vinegar
	salt
	pepper
7 oz/200 g	feta, in a piece

For the bell pepper coulis:

3	yellow bell peppers
3	red bell peppers
3	green bell peppers
⅔ cup/150 ml	olive oil
3 tbsp	red wine vinegar
3 cloves	garlic
	salt
	pepper

For the garnish:

	cilantro leaves
	cardamom leaves

This extremely elegant cold appetizer is a wonderful adaptation on the part of our chef. Drawing his inspiration from the famous eggplant caviar, he had the ingenious idea of dressing it with a trio of coulis made from bell peppers in three different colors. This delicious summer dish will not fail to delight the taste buds of all gourmets.

An essential ingredient in Greek cookery, the eggplant can be prepared in a number of ways. It combines wonderfully well with other ingredients. A native plant of India, by the Byzantine Age it had spread to Greece. An outstanding summer vegetable, it is now grown primarily in the Arcadia region of the country. It needs a soil that is rich in organic matter, and thrives in hot, humid conditions.

For this recipe, it is essential to prick the skins of the eggplants all over before they are put under the broiler. This dish, however, is traditionally cooked over the grill of a barbecue, when they absorb the aromas of the smoke. Choose small eggplants that don't contain any seeds.

This colorful dish is served with a trio of coulis, each made from a different color of bell pepper. Great mounds of peppers, the fruit of the capsicum plant, can be found in Greek markets when the days get warmer. The red variety is particularly popular for its sweetness. The stronger tasting green ones have a thick flesh and are slightly piquant, while the yellow or orange ones are, again, fairly sweet.

Sotiris Evangelou loves using regional produce so it's no surprise to find the famous feta cheese starring in this dish. Exported throughout the world, feta is made from ewe's milk and is prized for its salty, slightly sharp taste. It has been produced for thousands of years, and later on, borrowed its name from the Italian *fette*, which refers to the fact that it is cut into "slices."

Arrange all the peppers on a baking sheet, drizzle with olive oil, and broil them for about 15 minutes. Peel them, cut in half, and remove the seeds. Using a round cookie cutter, cut out 8 circles of pepper. Reserve the trimmings.

Put the trimmings from the peppers into the food processor in separate color batches.

For each separate color of pepper, make a coulis by putting 3 tbsp olive oil, 1 tbsp red wine vinegar, 1 clove garlic, salt, and pepper into the food processor and purée. Pass the 3 coulis through a fine mesh strainer.

Trio of Bell Pepper Coulis

Using the tip of a knife, prick the skins of the eggplants. Put them under the broiler or over the barbecue for about 30 minutes. Skin them, sprinkle the flesh with lemon juice, and cut into small dice.

Tip the diced eggplant into a bowl. Finely chop the onion, crush the garlic and add both to the bowl with the thyme leaves, if using. Pour over the olive oil and vinegar. Season with salt and pepper and mix well.

Using the same shaped cutter, cut the feta into 4 rounds. Divide the eggplant mixture neatly between 4 plates, carefully top with a slice of pepper, a slice of feta, then another slice of pepper. Pour the coulis around the stack and garnish with the cilantro and cardamom leaves.

Feta

Preparation time: 20 minutes
Cooking time: 15 minutes
Difficulty: ☆

Serves 4

4	tomatoes
2 cloves	garlic
1 bunch	basil
1 lb 2 oz/500 g	feta
7 or 8	black olives
1	red bell pepper

1 pinch	paprika
1 pinch	oregano
	olive oil

Saganaki are small pieces of grilled cheese, cooked in the oven in a metal dish of the same name. Extremely simple to make, they are both delicious and very colorful.

The internationally famous feta, a cheese made from ewe's milk which has been known to Greeks for several thousand years, is used in this dish. In *The Odyssey*, Homer refers to a ewe's milk cheese similar to today's feta. The Ancient Greek dramatist, Aristophanes, in his play *The Horseman* (400 B.C.) also refers to *chlorotyri* and *trophalyda*. Cut into slices before being packed into barrels, by the 17th century it had taken the name *feta*, a corruption of the Italian word *fette* or "slice." Without its rind, it is white and soft and can easily be cut into small cubes or slices. Providing it is kept well wrapped up and moistened with its brine, feta can keep for about six months in the refrigerator.

This dish is garnished with tomatoes, garlic, basil, feta, pepper and black olives, and should be generously sprinkled with olive oil, which will lend its flavor and prevent the other ingredients from sticking to the bottom of the cooking dish. For this recipe, our chef prefers to use the delicious olive oil from Sitia on the island of Crete. Greenish-yellow in color, this virgin oil has a very low acidity level and a fruity flavor. Its quality is due in great part to the amount of sun the crop receives and the specific composition of the local soil. Harvested at the end of November, the olives are pressed within three days of being picked.

Our chef normally prepares the *saganaki* in small individual dishes and tops each serving with a big piece of cheese. But as we have done here, you can also make it for several people in one large dish. The small cubes of golden feta will give the dish a more decorative appearance and provide a good showcase for all the other ingredients.

Wash the tomatoes and pat them dry. Cut each one into 3 thick slices.

Arrange the sliced tomatoes in a small ovenproof dish. Scatter over thin slices of peeled garlic and basil leaves.

Arrange 2 cubes of feta on top of each round of tomato.

Saganaki

Pit and halve the olives. Wash and dry the pepper. Slice it in half and remove the white membrane and seeds. Cut it into strips.

Arrange the strips of pepper among the tomatoes, with the feta on top. Scatter the black olives over the dish.

Sprinkle the top of the dish with paprika and oregano and drizzle with olive oil. Place the dish in an oven preheated to 475° F/240° C for 15 minutes. Garnish with a few basil leaves.

Filled Zucchini

Preparation time: 30 minutes
Cooking time: 10 minutes
Difficulty: ★

Serves 4

12	zucchini flowers
8 oz/225 g	feta
9 oz/250 g	grated dried *myzithra* cheese
	salt
	pepper
3	eggs

1 tbsp	chopped mint
1¾ cups/225 g	all-purpose flour
2 cups/500 ml	milk
4 cups/1 l	olive oil

Serving suggestions:

	cucumber
	plain yogurt
	fresh fennel
1	red bell pepper

Extremely popular throughout Greece, stuffed fried zucchini flowers make a wonderful summer dish. There are various recipes, and the flowers are often served with rice cooked in vegetable stock, stuffed with different Greek cheeses, such as feta and *myzithra*, and aromatic herbs.

The succulent flowers of the zucchini are 4–6 inches/10–15 centimeters long. They are often sold while still attached to the baby zucchini from which they have sprouted. To ensure that they don't wilt quickly, always keep them wrapped in plastic wrap in the refrigerator.

The filling we are going to use is a combination of two cheeses: feta and *myzithra*. Feta is made from either ewe's milk or goat's milk from which the curds are separated, and then poured into molds through which they can drain. After being cut into slices, the feta is salted then put into barrels where it is left to marinate in whey or brine.

Myzithra, meanwhile, is a by-product from the manufacture of feta or *kefalotyri*. After heating, the whey that results from straining the curds produces a sort of paste that is then strained again into spherical or flattened cone-shaped molds before being salted. *Myzithra* is either sold fresh or in a dried version that can be grated like parmesan.

To fry the zucchini flowers, our chef advises that you use a shallow pan because it will be easier to control the cooking and the browning. When they have turned light golden brown on one side, gently turn them over in the oil.

One attractive way of decorating the serving plates is to cut cucumber into petal shaped wedges. These can then be hollowed out and filled with yogurt flavored with finely chopped cucumber and decorated with sprigs of fresh fennel and strips of red bell pepper. A fresh zucchini flower in the center of the plate will add the ultimate gastronomic touch.

Detach the flowers from the baby zucchini. Rinse the flowers and gently pat dry.

Make the filling by mixing the feta, myzithra, salt, pepper, and 1 egg in a bowl. Add the freshly chopped mint.

Pick up a zucchini flower by its tip and open the petals. Using a teaspoon, place the filling in the center of the flower then fold the petals back over. Fill the other flowers in the same way.

Flowers

For the batter, sift the flour into a shallow bowl, add 2 eggs, salt, pepper, and the milk. Whisk until the batter is smooth and thick.

Using a fork, dip each stuffed zucchini flower into the batter, turning it to ensure it is well coated. Set aside on a plate.

Heat the olive oil in a large skillet. Place the flowers with their coating of batter into the hot oil. When they start to brown turn them over so that they are a uniform color. Drain them on paper towels and serve warm.

Broiled Vegetables

Preparation time: *10 minutes*
Cooking time: *20 minutes*
Difficulty: ✴

Serves 4

2	red bell peppers
2	green bell peppers
2	yellow bell peppers
2	medium eggplants
3	zucchini
	salt
	olive oil
2	sliced tomatoes (optional)

2 cloves	garlic
	flat-leaf parsley
7 oz/200 g	feta
	capers (optional)
1 pinch	dried oregano
	wine vinegar

In their restaurant, which is dedicated to the god Apollo, Konstantinos and Chrysanthi Stamkopoulos, invite their guests to discover the delights of traditional Greek dishes. This mix of broiled peppers, eggplants, and zucchini drizzled with olive oil has its near equivalent all around the Mediterranean.

Enjoyed hot or cold, broiled vegetables are a popular summer *mezze* throughout Greece. Food-lovers sometimes add a few well-ripened tomatoes to the griddle pan with some garlic, then use them to top the other vegetables.

The Greek name for the eggplant is *melitzana*, although it was unknown to the Ancient Greeks and Romans. In those days it was only grown in India, arriving in Greece via the Turks. These days this highly dietetic vegetable finds its way into much Greek cooking, whether broiled, puréed or made into little fritters.

The eggplant that is most highly prized in all Greece is the one grown in Tsakonia. Oblong in shape and pale mauve in color, it was first grown in the Arcadia region of the Peloponnese. This is followed by the popular and widely used eggplant grown in Komotini (Thrace), again oblong, but this time with a dark purple skin.

Unpeeled eggplants and zucchini can be cut into long thin slices and broiled, or grilled over a charcoal barbecue or on a cast iron griddle.

The Greeks usually use long slim peppers to make this dish, which they leave whole after broiling. If you are using big bell peppers, cut them into thick strips instead.

After arranging the vegetables on the plate, all you need to do is add the feta, herbs, vinaigrette, and a few capers for that touch of extravagance.

Wash and dry the peppers. Arrange them on a baking sheet and put them under the broiler for about 20 minutes or until the skins have turned black and wrinkled. In the meantime, cut the unpeeled eggplants and zucchini lengthwise.

Line up the eggplants and zucchini on a cutting board. Sprinkle with salt and brush with olive oil. Sprinkle with salt again, then cook on a cast-iron griddle, with the tomato slices, if using.

When the peppers are done, remove them from the heat and leave to cool before carefully peeling them with your fingers or a small knife.

Konstantinos Style

Split the peppers. Using the tip of your knife, remove all the little seeds and the membrane. Cut the flesh first into big pieces then into strips.

Peel the garlic and cut it into very thin slivers. Finely chop the parsley. On the serving plate, arrange alternating layers of eggplant, strips of multicolored peppers, and the zucchini.

Decorate the vegetables with the slivers of garlic, crumbled feta, and capers, if using. Sprinkle with chopped parsley and dried oregano, then drizzle with vinaigrette made from olive oil and wine vinegar.

Greek-style

Preparation time:	40 minutes
Cooking time:	15 minutes
Soaking time (cod roe):	12 hours
Difficulty:	☆

Serves 4

For the tzatziki:

½	cucumber
1 cup/250 g	Greek, or thick creamy, yogurt
5 cloves	garlic
1¼ cups/300 ml	olive oil
½ bunch	dill
	salt
	pepper

For the taramasalata:

5½ oz/150 g	cod roe (soaked)
1	onion

3½ oz/100 g	white breadcrumbs
3½ tbsp	olive oil
1	lemon
	black pepper

For the ktipiti:

1	red bell pepper
1	yellow bell pepper
9 oz/250 g	feta
½ bunch	dill
3 stems	chives
½	lemon
2 tbsp	olive oil
1 tbsp	*boukovo* (dried, flaked pimento)
3 tsp	dried cilantro
1 tsp	cumin

Found on most Greek tables, these *mezze*, or appetizers, are classics in the country's gastronomic repertoire. Generously offered to guests, these bright sunny dishes are enjoyed with a glass of ouzo, the strong national alcoholic drink flavored with aniseed. They are very easy to make and are ideal for sharing with friends when it's time for an aperitif.

These days the word *tarama* has entered the universal language of cookery, but for newcomers it means a savory cream made with the eggs of mullet or cod. For Greeks, though, it means something different. In fact for the inhabitants of this magnificent country bordered by the sea, the word *tarama* only refers to the basic ingredient (fish eggs) and not to the dish itself.

Intransigent about the quality of this seafood dish, our chef strongly recommends that you use white cod roe. Because it is very salty, it is essential that the cod roe be left for several hours in a bowl filled with water before use. Once the cod roe has been mixed with the bread, onion, lemon, olive oil, and black pepper, this outstanding dish takes the name *taramasalata*!

In Greece, a tray of *mezze* always includes deliciously refreshing dips and snacks. There are many similarities between *tzatziki* and the popular Turkish dish, *cacık*. Made from yogurt, garlic, cucumber, olive oil, dill, salt, and pepper, it is often served with broiled meat kebabs or squid.

A testament to the richness of Mediterranean cuisine, *mezze* go with anything. Our chef would also like to introduce you to a summer salad based on peppers grown in the Thessalonika area. Bursting with Greek flavors, the wonderful *ktipiti* brings out the tart taste of the famous feta, which was already being produced in the days of Homer.

For the tzatziki, peel strips off the cucumber so you are left with a striped pattern along its length. Then grate it and strain off any liquid.

Tip the yogurt into a salad bowl. Peel and crush the cloves of garlic and add them together with the olive oil and the chopped dill to the bowl. Add the cucumber. Season with salt and pepper and mix well. Spoon the taztziki into a little dish.

For the taramasalata, leave the cod roe to soak in water for 12 hours. Drain well. Put it into a food processor with the chopped onion and breadcrumbs and blend finely.

Mezze

Pour the olive oil into the processor with lemon juice. Add some black pepper and blend. Spoon the taramasalata into a small dish.

To make the ktipiti, broil the peppers for 15 minutes. Peel them and finely dice one half and cut the other half into strips. Reserve the strips for garnishing.

In a salad bowl mix the diced peppers with crumbled feta, chopped dill, and snipped chives. Pour in the lemon juice and the olive oil. Sprinkle with boukovo, cilantro, and cumin. Serve garnished with strips of pepper.

Mezze of Fried Vegetables

Preparation time: 40 minutes
Cooking time: 15 minutes
Difficulty: ★

Serves 4

4	zucchini
4	tomatoes
2	eggplants
12 oz/350 g	potatoes
6 tbsp/50 g	all-purpose flour
1 cup/250 ml	olive oil for frying

	salt
½–¾ cup/150 g	Greek, or thick and creamy, yogurt
1 bunch	mint
	olive oil
	pepper
5½ oz/150 g	feta

For the garnish:

mint leaves

In the Greek culinary repertoire, the word *mezze* means a whole range of small dishes in bright sunny colors. A symbol of hospitality, these appetizers are enjoyed among friends, generally accompanied by a glass of ouzo, the national drink of Greece, with its distinctive aniseed taste.

Highly prized by Greeks, fried vegetables served with a sauce made from yogurt are particularly popular when served at tavernas in the summer. This dish draws its fruity flavor from the olive oil, and its mix of potatoes, zucchini, and eggplant is sheer magic for the taste buds. Panagiotis Delvenakiotis recommends that you use extra-virgin olive oil for this dish. Obtained from one single cold pressing, this olive oil is sought out for its powerful taste.

This *mezze* is served with a very refreshing sauce. The mint releases its full aroma when judiciously married with the yogurt. In Ancient Greece, mint was well-known for its

stimulating properties. Rich in iron, calcium, and vitamins, it was believed to bring power, peace, and to help healing.

Green mint, known as *diosmos*, is found all over Thrace and western Macedonia. Its elongated or oval leaves, smooth or toothed, are found all year round on market stalls. If you want to keep it fresh, put it in a plastic bag and store it in the refrigerator.

Greek tradition calls for generous numbers and portions of *mezze* to be served at the table, so everyone can then help themselves to whatever they like from the different dishes. Our chef decided to enrich the fried vegetables with a delicious tomato and feta salad. Internationally known, this specialty brings together typically Greek flavors, and all of your guests will leave happy.

Wash and dry the zucchini, tomatoes, and eggplants. Peel the potatoes. Cut all the vegetables into thin round slices of equal thickness.

Carefully coat the slices of zucchini and eggplant with the flour.

Heat some olive oil in a skillet. Add the slices of zucchini and fry on both sides then remove and blot with paper towels. Sprinkle with salt.

Florina Peppers

Arrange the peppers on a serving plate and scatter over the capers.

Prepare the garlic vinaigrette in a bowl by mixing the remaining olive oil with the chopped garlic, large pinch of salt, oregano, and vinegar, and whisking everything together.

Drizzle the garlic vinaigrette over the peppers and eat them when they have completely cooled.

Icaria Octopus Cooked

Preparation time:	*25 minutes*
Cooking time :	*30 minutes*
Marinating time (octopus):	*30 minutes*
Difficulty:	☆

Serves 6

1	octopus weighing 2¼ lb/1 kg
	salt
scant ½ cup/ 100 ml	red wine vinegar
3½ oz/100 g	red bell peppers
3½ oz/100 g	green bell peppers
3 tbsp	capers

2 cloves	garlic
2 tsp	dried oregano
1 handful	fresh fennel leaves
1 cup/250 ml	extra-virgin olive oil

Located in the eastern part of the Aegean Sea and close to the Turkish coast, the island of Icaria, set in crystal clear waters, has retained its wild landscapes, thermal springs, and numerous vestiges of past civilizations, some of which date back to the Neolithic Age. From April to October the seas around the island teem with all sorts of marine life.

In their natural environment, octopuses live close to the rocks. The locals sometimes spear them in the craggy places where they hide. Since industrial fishing for octopus is unknown on the Greek Islands, the fishermen who capture them sell them direct to local restaurants. There they are made into the famous recipe for octopus that our chef has updated for you.

When choosing an octopus, Miltos Karoubas recommends that you look for one with firm flesh and plump tentacles, weighing less than 5 ½ pounds/2.5 kilograms. It is best, in fact, to avoid the heavier ones, which are older and thus have flesh that has become soggy and spongy.

The addition of vinegar to the cooking water makes the flesh turn a very appetizing deep red color. Note that Greek chefs also use this method for poaching shrimp and spiny lobster. To check whether it's done, you need to prick the flesh of the octopus several times with a fork. When the fork goes in easily, the octopus is cooked.

This recipe is generally served on small plates set out in the middle of the table alongside other small dishes such as *taramasalata* or *tzatziki*. The marinade should fill half the plate so that the octopus is bathed in it. Do as the Greeks do and mop up the sauce with a piece of bread.

Wash the octopus. Plunge it into a large pan filled with salted water. Add 3–4 tbsp red wine vinegar. Bring the pan to the boil and cook for 30 minutes, adding more water if necessary. Drain the octopus and cut it into thick slices.

Slice open the peppers, remove the seeds and white membrane and cut the flesh into fine julienne strips.

In a metal bowl mix the pieces of octopus, the strips of pepper, and the capers.

the Karoubas Way

Add 1 clove of garlic, peeled and finely chopped, to the dried oregano and the chopped fennel leaves and mix.

Make a garlic vinaigrette in a bowl by whisking together the olive oil, remaining wine vinegar, the other peeled and chopped garlic clove, and a pinch of salt.

Pour the garlic vinaigrette over the octopus and the peppers. Mix well. Leave to marinate for 30 minutes then eat when it has thoroughly cooled.

Prasopita

Preparation time: 20 minutes
Cooking time: 50 minutes
Difficulty: ★

Serves 6

6	leeks
scant ½ cup/ 100 ml	olive oil
1 bunch	dill
2	bay leaves
½ cup/50 g	coarse semolina
	salt
	pepper

3	eggs
1 scant cup/ 100 g	grated Gruyère (or *kasseri* cheese)
2–3 tbsp	dried breadcrumbs
7 oz/200 g	feta

Born in Kozani, a district of western Macedonia, Chrysanthi Stamkopoulos has prepared *prasopita* for you, a sort of "flat cake" made with leeks, which her grandmother used to make. This is a very nourishing dish that is altogether simpler than the pies made with phyllo (filo) pastry.

Since leeks are a winter vegetable, *prasopita* is particularly prized during that season. Within mainland Greece there are still many little villages where everybody cultivates their own vegetable gardens and whose diets therefore follow the seasons. Grown for thousands of years, the leek was highly esteemed by the Assyrians, Egyptians, and the Hebrews. The best warriors of the Pharaoh Cheops were all rewarded – with armfuls of leeks!

Leeks are often used to help shore up the soil and to rid it of various impurities. After cutting the leeks into slices, put them into a colander and wash them in an abundant supply of fresh running water. Raw, leeks keep for five days in the refrigerator, providing that the top part of the leaves has first been cut off.

Enriched with aromatic herbs and eggs, the leeks used for the *prasopita* can also be accompanied with thin slivers of carrot and garlic. The grated cheese, whether Gruyère or *kasseri*, will also add to the flavor, help to bind the mixture, and give it a softer, smoother texture. For a more authentic taste, use *kasseri*, a cheese made from ewe's milk or cow's milk produced in Thessalia, central Greece, and in in the northern Aegean. Pale yellow in color, it has a soft consistency and no rind. The flavor is soft and salty.

Our chef generally pours the mix into a large rectangular mold, the base covered with dried breadcrumbs to prevent the *prasopita* from sticking to the bottom. A circular mold has been used here.

Trim off the tough green part and the root of the leeks. Slice the white and the light green parts into rounds. Rinse them thoroughly in a colander under running water to make sure that any soil is removed.

In a saucepan, gently fry the leeks for 5 minutes in a little hot oil. Add the chopped dill and bay leaves and stir for about 10 minutes over the heat. Remove the bay leaves, add the semolina, and mix again. Season with salt and pepper.

Whisk the eggs in a separate bowl. Add to the leek mixture and stir well.

Kozanis

Reduce the heat to low and stir in the grated Gruyère or kasseri cheese.

Sprinkle the bottom of an ovenproof dish with the dried breadcrumbs and, using a spatula, transfer the leek mixture into the dish.

Arrange small cubes of feta at regular intervals over the surface of the dish. Cook in an oven preheated to 425° F/220° C for 30 minutes and serve piping hot.

Greek

| Preparation: | 25 minutes |
| Difficulty: | ✳ |

Serves 4

4	small cucumbers
4	tomatoes
2	medium onions
1 each	green, red, and yellow
	bell peppers
1 bunch	flat-leaf parsley
1 bunch	arugula (rocket)
8 oz/225 g	feta

24	black Kalamata olives
	olive oil
	salt
1 pinch	oregano
	capers (optional)

Greek salad, which we present here in its most traditional form, is frequently found among the assortment of dishes that make up the *mezze* served with aperitifs. It is served with *tzatziki*, marinated octopus, broiled bell peppers, or stuffed vine leaves. Everybody likes to relax with these fresh and appetizing dishes, washed down with a glass of ouzo.

In restaurants this salad is always served in copious quantities, but rarely as a dish on its own. As well as an accompaniment to an aperitif, the Greeks enjoy eating this crunchy and juicy salad with broiled lamb.

Cucumbers, or *angouri*, are refreshing and low in calories and are used in many local appetizers. Mixed with yogurt and garlic, cucumber is transformed into *tzatziki*, a flavorsome creamy dip. Greek cooks traditionally use small and highly aromatic cucumbers.

Our salad is enriched with black Kalamata olives, which have a more robust taste. Grown in the Massini area of the Peloponnese, these oval shaped fruits are picked by hand then split in two with a razor blade before being covered with brine to impregnate them with salt. If you prefer, you can use green olives instead.

Greek salad is sometimes known as *horiatiki salata* ("rustic salad"). Cooks from different areas like to add local wild herbs, but romaine lettuce can also be used. Some like to add boiled potatoes or hard-cooked eggs. Likewise the feta can be replaced by fresh goat milk cheese.

Like the Greeks, take care not to mix all the vegetables together and season them in a bowl before you serve them. Instead, arrange your ingredients artistically directly onto the serving plate so as to preserve their color, flavor, and individual crispness. Season and serve immediately.

Peel the cucumbers. Cut them in half lengthwise, then into thin half-moon slices.

Wash the tomatoes, cut them in half and then into segments. Peel the onions then slice into thin rings.

Wash the peppers. Cut them open across the middle. Remove the seeds and the white membrane and slice into fine rings.

Salad

Wash the parsley and arugula and roughly chop with a knife.

On the serving platter, arrange the parsley, arugula and cucumbers around the edge, then the peppers, tomatoes and cubes of feta in the center, and the slices of onion around the outer edges.

Scatter over the olives and add a generous drizzle of olive oil, salt to taste, a pinch of oregano, and the capers, if using.

Green Salad with Mussels

Preparation time:	40 minutes
Cooking time:	5 minutes
Salting time (anchovies):	2 hours
Marinating time (anchovies):	1 hour
Difficulty:	✶

Serves 4

7 oz/200 g	fresh anchovies
7 oz/200 g	sea salt
10 oz/300 g	mussels
2 cloves	garlic
3–4 tbsp	white wine
5	whole peppercorns
7 oz/200 g	baby spinach

2	romaine lettuce
1	frisée lettuce
2 bunches	arugula (rocket)
3–4 tbsp	olive oil
3–4 tbsp	ouzo
1	lemon
	salt, pepper

For the marinade:

3–4 tbsp	olive oil
1 bunch	dill
2	lemons

For the garnish:

1	tomato

Extremely refreshing, this green salad with mussels and small, marinated anchovies is a traditional recipe from the north of the island of Eubea. Encircled by the Aegean Sea, this piece of land, split off from the flank of Attica, is famous for its fish dishes.

Easy to make, this appetizer, which can be enjoyed both cold or warm, is full of typically Greek flavors. The mussels, when prepared like this, are impregnated with the aniseed flavor of ouzo, the national drink of Greece. In other regions they are often served fried with a tomato sauce.

We strongly advise you to be extra careful when selecting mussels. Throw away any that are closed or have broken shells. Before cooking them, clean thoroughly by scraping off the beards and then scrubbing thoroughly under running water. If you are planning to use ready-cooked mussels, you can just drop them directly into the hot olive oil.

This summer salad is a treat for lovers of anchovies. Known as *gavros* in Greek, these little fish are highly prized by Mediterranean people. Measuring no more than 8 inches/20 centimeters long, they can be recognized by their greenish-blue backs and silver sides. They must always be kept in the refrigerator. If you find it difficult to fillet them, your fishmonger may be persuaded to do it for you, some delicatessens have them already prepared.

Under no circumstances should the anchovies be left to salt for more than two hours. The time for which they can be marinated, on the other hand, can be quite a lot longer than the one hour suggested here. Marinating the fish gives them a naturally aromatic taste and at the same time helps preserve them in perfect shape.

Nikos Sarandos suggests replacing the green salad with young Swiss chard leaves that have first been blanched.

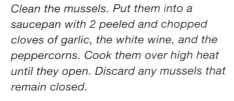

Open out the anchovy fillets with your fingers, making sure you have removed the heads first. Sprinkle them all over with sea salt. Leave them for a maximum of 2 hours.

Clean the mussels. Put them into a saucepan with 2 peeled and chopped cloves of garlic, the white wine, and the peppercorns. Cook them over high heat until they open. Discard any mussels that remain closed.

Wash and dry the spinach, the romaine and frisée lettuces, and the arugula. Tear the leaves into pieces and set aside.

and Marinated Anchovies

Wash the salt off the anchovy fillets in clean water. Blot dry and arrange them on a dish. Let them marinade for about 1 hour in 3–4 tbsp olive oil, the chopped dill, and the juice of 2 lemons.

Shell the mussels. Strain the cooking liquid and set aside.

Heat 3–4 tbsp olive oil in a skillet and add the mussels. Pour in the ouzo, lemon juice, and 2 tbsp cooking liquid. Season and warm it through. Arrange a pile of salad leaves on a serving plate, and top with the mussels and anchovies. Garnish with slices of tomato.

Mytilene

Preparation time:	30 minutes
Cooking time:	50 minutes
Total draining time (zucchini):	1 hour
Difficulty:	✳

Serves 6

4½ lb/2 kg	zucchini
4 or 5	zucchini flowers
3½ oz/100 g	bacon
2	medium onions

scant ½ cup/ 100 ml	olive oil
1 lb 5 oz/600 g	feta
12	eggs
	mint leaves
1 bunch	dill

Many of the poets and musicians of Greek Antiquity were born on the island of Lesbos, also known as Mytilene. These days, the third biggest Greek island still retains vestiges of its past – antiquities, Byzantine ruins, and little picturesque fishing harbors.

In the olden days, the diet of the people living on the Greek islands comprised vegetables, wild herbs, cheese, olive oil, and bread because meat was so rare and expensive. This is reflected in *sfougato*, literally a "flat cake," made from eggs flavored with herbs, enriched with fresh and natural ingredients.

Look for small, tender and delicately scented baby zucchini that still have their pretty orange flowers. If the flowers have not been "cleaned," remove the central pistil. Some cooks also make *sfougato* with potatoes or spinach.

The feta made on the island of Mytilene is prized throughout the whole of Greece. Although this cheese was made in ancient times, the word *feta* only dates from the 17th-century Venetian occupation. In Venetian, *fette* means "slice" because the cheese is cut into slices before being put into a brine solution. A word of advice: Don't bother with the insipid feta produced on an industrial scale using cow's milk.

The inhabitants of Mytilene also produce a very famous olive oil. Bright golden yellow in color, it has the sort of flavor characteristic of fully ripe olives.

Cooks on Mytilene traditionally cook pork at Christmas. They smoke some parts of the pig, and make full use of any meat left over as a filling for the *sfougato*. This can be replaced by bacon or cubes of pancetta. Unlike an omelet, the *sfougato* is not folded but has the shape of a "flat cake" that is served directly from the dish in which it was cooked.

Quickly grate the unpeeled zucchini using a grater with large holes. Then leave them to drain for 30 minutes in a colander.

Arrange the zucchini flowers on a cutting board. Cut them into pieces measuring about ½ in/1 cm square. Cut the bacon into very small cubes. Peel and chop the onions.

Heat the oil in a skillet, fry the bacon and the onions for 5 minutes, then add the grated zucchini. Leave to cook for 5–10 minutes, stirring all the time, then pour the mixture into a colander and leave to drain for 30 minutes.

Sfougato

Put the mixture into a bowl. Add the pieces of zucchini flower and roughly crumbled feta.

In another bowl, whisk the eggs and add chopped mint and dill. Pour this mixture into the zucchini–feta mix. Mix well with a wooden spatula.

Pour the prepared mixture into a large gratin dish. Cook in a preheated moderate oven at 325° F/170° C for 30–35 minutes. Serve hot or cold.

Spetzofai

Preparation time:	35 minutes
Cooking time:	1 hour
Difficulty:	★

Serves 4

5	green bell peppers
5	red bell peppers
2	eggplants
½–⅔ cup/130 ml	olive oil
1 lb 2 oz/500 g	pork and beef sausages

3	onions
3½ oz/100 g	tomatoes
	salt
	pepper
1 tsp	dried oregano
½ tsp	boukovo (dried flaked pimento)

For the garnish:

parsley

Originally from Volos and now an extremely popular dish in Greece, *spetzofai* literally means, in the local dialect, "meal based on peppers." Situated between Thessalonika and Athens, this charming coastal town with its narrow, busy streets leading down to the harbor has had a prestigious past. According to legend, it was from Iolkos, just outside Volos, that Jason set sail on board the Argus, in search of the fabled Golden Fleece.

Spetzofai is usually served as a main course, although it is sometimes also eaten as a warm appetizer. Bursting with Mediterranean flavors, this specialty is easy to make and marries the sun-ripened vegetables with the sausages in a wonderful way.

Commonly called *piperia* in Greek, the bell pepper, which is the real star of this recipe, is also known in the Volos region as *spetzo*. This precious fruit of the capsicum, brought from the New World in the 16th century, has rapidly found its place in the various cuisines of Southern Europe. In this dish, red and green bell peppers are used together to wonderful effect. The red ones, deprived of bitterness, lend their smooth taste and sweet flavor. The green ones confirm their well-known reputation.

Even though the name of the dish celebrates the peppers, we must not forget the contribution of the eggplant. Highly prized in Greece, it is the basic ingredient in many special Greek recipes, including the famous moussaka. Choose ones that have unblemished smooth and firm skins. The stalk should be as fresh as possible.

Typically Greek, *boukovo*, dried red pimento flakes, is famous for its powerful punch. Picked from the first days of summer onward, the fruits are delivered to the cooperative where they are dried and flaked in a special type of grinder.

Broil the green and red peppers for about 30 minutes. Dip them into cold water and peel. Remove the seeds and membrane, and cut the flesh into thick slices.

Slice off the top of the eggplants and peel them in strips to achieve a striped effect. Cut into cubes of equal thickness.

Heat a scant ½ cup/100 ml olive oil in a skillet. Add the cubes of eggplant and allow them to brown. Remove and pat dry on paper towels.

from Volos

Cut the sausages into cubes. Heat 2 tbsp/30 ml olive oil in a skillet and fry the sausages. Remove and pat dry on paper towels.

Finely dice the onions and chop the tomatoes. In the same skillet, add more oil if necessary, and fry onions. Add the tomatoes and a little water. Season to taste and cook for 10–15 minutes.

Arrange the peppers, eggplant, and sausage in an ovenproof dish. Sprinkle with oregano and boukovo, and pour over the tomato and onion sauce. Cook in an oven preheated to 400° F/200° C for 30 minutes. Use a serving slice to serve the spetzofai and garnish with parsley.

Canea Lamb

Preparation time: 50 minutes
Cooking time: 1 hour
20 minutes
Resting time (pastry): 20 minutes
Difficulty: ★

Serves 4

1¾ lb/800 g	leg of lamb (boned)
	salt, pepper
½ bunch	mint
1 lb 2 oz/500 g	*anthotyros* cheese
10 oz/300 g	*malaka* cheese
1 sprig	thyme
1 sprig	oregano
1 tsp	dried marjoram

2	lemons
1 tbsp	olive oil
1	egg yolk (glaze)
2 tbsp	sesame seeds

For the pastry:

¾ cup/200 ml	milk
½ oz/20 g	fresh yeast (or 1½ tsp dried)
1 lb 5 oz/600 g	all-purpose flour
2 oz/50 g	lamb suet
2	eggs
	salt

For the garnish:

mint leaves

A favorite in the little coastal town of Canea, this lamb pie is a Cretan specialty. This "puff pastry" dish is particularly popular at weddings.

Cretan cooking is very healthy, and even today it retains many similarities with the Minoan civilization. One text dating from 1800 B.C. was already referring to a dish made from lamb wrapped in pastry.

Renowned for its exceptional taste, lamb has been the meat of choice since the days of Ancient Greece. Sheep are raised in the mountainous regions of the country, where they graze on wild grasses, and the meat takes on a wonderfully aromatic taste. Depending on the season, this recipe can also be made with kid goat.

Carefully thought out, this pie is a wonderful mix of aromatic herbs. It is a reflection of Crete itself, where thyme, mint, oregano, and rosemary all grow in abundance – this dish only serving to magnify their typically Mediterranean flavors. A close cousin of oregano, the subtlety of marjoram shines through in this puff pastry pie. Originally from Asia, this herb is used in Greece to add extra flavor to various meats and marinades. If you want to dry it, cut the stems just before the plant comes into flower.

A substantial dish, Canea lamb pie is further enriched by a filling made from three different types of cheese. Typically Greek, *anthotyros*, made from ewe's milk or goat's milk, was in the olden days known as *myzithra* in Crete. *Malaka*, meanwhile, is an unsalted, fully skimmed soft cheese that was mentioned as long ago as the 6th century in documents found on the island of Santorini. You can easily replace the *anthotyros* with Gruyère and the *malaka* with mozzarella.

Put the boned leg of lamb into a saucepan. Season with the salt and pepper, cover with water and simmer over moderate heat for about 40 minutes. Strain the stock and set aside. Cut the meat into small pieces.

To make the pastry, first warm the milk. Add the yeast and leave to rise (if using dried yeast, follow maker's instructions). Sift the flour into a large bowl and add the suet, eggs, and salt. Make a well and gradually mix in the milk, then work by hand.

Pour a scant ½ cup/100 ml lamb stock onto the pastry mix. Continue to knead, then leave to rest for 20 minutes.

Pie

On a floured board, roll out the pastry thinly. Finely chop the mint and mix with the anthotyros and malaka cheeses. Season with salt.

Mix the lamb pieces with the herb leaves. Add the lemon juice. Oil the base and sides of an ovenproof dish and line with the pastry, leaving long overhangs of pastry. Spread the mint and cheese filling on the pastry base. Spread the meat evenly on top and moisten with a little stock.

Fold the pastry back over to form a lid for the pie. Beat the egg yolk and use it to glaze the top of the pie. Sprinkle with sesame seeds. Cook in an oven preheated to 300° F/150° C for 40 minutes. Serve garnished with mint leaves.

Soups

Kakavia

Preparation time:	50 minutes
Cooking time:	20 minutes
Difficulty:	★

Serves 4

1	sea bream weighing 1½ lb/600 g
1	scorpion fish weighing 1½ lb/600 g
1	eel
2	onions
1¾ lb/800 g	potatoes
	salt

	pepper
⅔ cup/150 ml	olive oil
2 cups/500 ml	white wine
2	lemons
2	quinces
3–4 cloves	garlic
	fennel leaves

For the garnish:
fresh dill

To serve:
toasted chunks of bread

Kakavia is a delicious soup that is traditionally eaten by fishermen. Extremely popular in Greece, this cousin of bouillabaisse from Marseille in southern France takes its name from the *kakavin*, a cooking pot that was used by sailors in the olden days to cook the different fish they caught in their nets.

Bursting with unrivaled flavors, this soup is still made today on board the small boats that sail around the Greek islands, and they still use seawater! According to our chef, the inhabitants of the Greek islands also traditionally make it once a year when they celebrate their local patron saint.

Kakavia pays homage to the Mediterranean Sea and can be made from all kinds of fish, depending on the catch. Aristedes Pasparakis has used scorpion fish, always regarded as a great delicacy here. Known as *skorpios* in Greek, it is famous for its white, slightly oily, flesh.

This soup also stars the sea bream. This fish is most often found around the Mediterranean coast where it is prized for its taste and delicacy. But be extra careful when you cook it because its delicately flavored texture tends to become soft and a bit fluffy.

Over the years, local fishermen have started to introduce products from the New World into this dish. Potatoes, which originated in South America, today enrich the original recipe. On certain islands the appearance is further enlivened with the addition of tomato.

A judicious concoction of flavors, *kakavia* is served with chunks of toasted bread and a dish of *skordalia*, a sort of Greek aioli. Made from garlic, olive oil, quince, lemon juice, fennel leaves, salt, and pepper this "sauce" not only lifts but comes into its own with this tasty soup.

Scale and clean the sea bream and the scorpion fish. Fillet the fish. Reserve the heads for the stock. Cut the prepared eel into thick chunks.

Peel the onions and the potatoes and slice both into regular-shaped rounds.

Layer the onions on the bottom of the pan. Cover these with half the potatoes. Add the fillets of sea bream and the reserved fish heads.

Add the remaining potatoes, eel chunks, and the fillets of scorpion fish. Season to taste and add a scant half cup/100 ml olive oil, the white wine, and 4 cups/ 1 l water. Bring to the boil and cook for 15 minutes. Remove the fish heads and squeeze in the juice of 1 lemon.

Wash the quinces and cut in half. Drop them into a pan of boiling water and cook for about 15 minutes. Drain the quinces.

When cooled, peel the quinces and blend well in a processor with the garlic, juice of the second lemon, salt, and pepper. Add the fennel leaves and the remaining olive oil. Serve the kakavia, the quince sauce, and the toasted bread in separate bowls. Garnish with sprigs of dill.

Kreatosoupa

Preparation time:	30 minutes
Cooking time:	1 hour
	30 minutes
Difficulty:	★★

Serves 4

2¼ lb/1 kg	lean veal (from top of the leg)
	salt
	pepper
1 bunch	flat-leaf parsley
2	onions
3	carrots

3–4	potatoes
1	leek
2	small zucchini
1 stalk	celery
	olive oil

For the avgolemono sauce:

2	egg yolks
2	lemons
1 tbsp	cornstarch

Kreatosoupa is a popular family dish in Greece. This winter soup is made from veal or beef, boiled with carrots, celery, and potatoes. Just before it is served, it receives the ultimate Greek touch, the addition of *avgolemono*, a sauce made from eggs and lemons.

Even today, such a hearty soup is used as the main meal of the day in Greek households. It is often made with meat stock prepared with leftover scraps of meat and fresh vegetables, sometimes thickened with pulses, potatoes, or rice. It is often enriched with the *avgolemono*, but just simple lemon juice can be used.

To make this soup we have chosen to use veal from the top of the leg, an excellent lean, tender meat with a fine grain which can be used in many different ways – roasted, cut into thin slices, larded and braised, or as escalopes. After purchase, it can be kept for two or three days in the coldest part of the refrigerator, but be careful to leave it at room temperature for 30 minutes before you cook it. If it is too cold, it doesn't cook well. To prepare the veal, cut off any fat and remove the small nerves. Greek cooks always rinse it well before they cut it.

After the meat has been cooking for about 12 minutes, a lot of froth starts to form on top of the cooking liquid. This needs to be regularly skimmed off and the skimming spoon must be washed every time.

The *avgolemono* is poured over the veal at the last minute. Our chef only uses egg yolks because the whites coagulate too quickly and separate into strands. Leave the stock to cool a little before adding it in a gentle stream to the lemon-eggs-cornstarch mix. If it is too hot, the eggs will "scramble" and not blend with the sauce. The cornstarch also helps bind the other ingredients used in the sauce.

Wash the veal and pat it dry. Cut the meat into chunks and then into approximately 1-in/2.5-cm cubes. Bring 4–6 cups/ 1–1½ l water to the boil in a large saucepan and season. Lower the heat, add the veal and let it cook for 45 minutes, regularly skimming off any froth.

Peel the onions, wash the parsley and trim off the stems, then chop the onions and parsley. Peel the carrots and potatoes. Trim the leek and remove the outer leaves. Cut the ends off the zucchini and the celery stalk. Cut the vegetables into rough chunks and rinse in a colander.

When the meat has been cooking for 45 minutes, add the prepared vegetables and herbs.

Add a dash of olive oil. Put a lid on the pan and continue cooking at a gentle, rolling boil for another 45 minutes.

To make the avgolemono sauce, whisk the egg yolks in a bowl with the lemon juice and cornstarch. Ladle out some of the cooking stock from the pan and, after it has cooled a little, pour it gradually on-to the lemon and eggs mixture, while whisking continuously.

Pour the resulting avgolemono into the pan of meat and vegetables. Reheat for 1–2 minutes, stirring all the time. Serve immediately.

Ntomatosoupa

Preparation time: 35 minutes
Cooking time: 50 minutes
Difficulty: ☆

Serves 4

9 lb/4 kg	ripe tomatoes
2 sprigs	basil
2	onions
1 clove	garlic
2 tbsp	olive oil
	salt
	black pepper

1 pinch	sugar
4½ oz/125 g	kritharaki (Greek noodles)
3–4 tbsp/50 g	Greek, or thick creamy, yogurt

Typical of the sort of food eaten at Greek monasteries, this tomato soup, *ntomatosoupa*, tastes of pure summer. Extremely refreshing, this light dish varies according to the part of Greece in which you eat it. In Athens they add *kritharaki*, typically Greek noodles, or even bulgur wheat. Others prefer simply to serve it with a yogurt sauce.

Extremely easy to make, *ntomatosoupa* awards the starring role to the tomato. Originally from Peru, this fruit was first imported to Spain in the 16th century, although it had to wait more than 200 years before it found its way onto Southern European tables. Tomatoes love the sun so they flourish in Mediterranean countries. In Greece the Cyclades islands produce a very small variety that are bright red and have a distinctive taste. These vegetables, which are ready to use very early in the year, are traditionally grown on non-irrigated land.

For this recipe, try to find the Roma, or plum, tomato. Firm fleshed and with a delicate flavor, this is an excellent "cooking" tomato. When you've removed the seeds, don't forget to keep them. Wrapped up in a cheesecloth with a few sprigs of basil, they can be added to the water used to flavor the soup.

The somewhat delicate flavor of this dish is lifted by the slightly sharp taste of the Greek yogurt. Creamy smooth and with a dense consistency, Greek yogurt is primarily made from ewe's milk. It is the inspiration behind many Greek specialties, including the famous *tzatziki*, a *mezze* dish based on cucumber and garlic.

The lovely yogurt sauce is enhanced with the aroma of basil. The leaves of this aromatic herb have been prized for thousands of years. Often served with tomatoes, they generously impart their strong flavor of lemon and jasmine.

Wash the tomatoes and cut into quarters. Remove the seeds, which should be kept to one side. Blend the tomatoes to a purée in the food processor.

Put the reserved seeds into a piece of cheesecloth. Add the basil stalks, stripped of the leaves, and tie the cloth into a pouch shape. Chop, or tear, the basil leaves and keep to one side.

Peel and finely chop the onions. Peel and crush the garlic. Brown both together in 1 tbsp olive oil. Add the tomato purée. Cover with about 4 cups/1 l water, season to taste, and add the sugar. Cook over a gentle heat for about 40 minutes.

Bring some water to a rolling boil in a small pan and drop in the pouch containing the tomato seeds and basil stalks. Cook for 10 minutes, remove the pouch, then pour the flavored water into the tomato soup.

Add the Greek noodles and cook for about 10 minutes.

In a small bowl, mix the Greek yogurt with 1 tbsp olive oil, season, and add the chopped basil leaves. Serve the soup in bowls topped with a spoonful of the yogurt sauce.

Potage of Lamb with

Preparation time: 30 minutes
Cooking time: 1 hour 20 minutes

Difficulty: ☆

Serves 4

1¾ lb/800g	shoulder of lamb
2 tbsp	all-purpose flour
3	eggs
3	lemons
1 small bunch	mint

Spices for cooking the lamb:

1	cinnamon stick
1 pinch	nutmeg
3	cloves
10	allspice berries
10	black peppercorns
	salt

In the heart of the Peloponnese, the mountains around Arcadia are famous for the sheep and goats that are raised there. They graze on the rich local plant life that gives their meat a distinct aromatic flavor. In our recipe, the meat is cooked in a stock made with different spices and enriched with lemon juice and eggs. When eaten for lunch, and especially on the evenings of public holidays, it is usually served with a pie made with herbs.

Greeks once regarded meat as a sacred food – ceremonies would be held during which animals were sacrificed. Nothing from the animal is ever wasted, the meat being so rare and precious, even when it is made into soup. The pieces of lamb are thus presented "complete" with their bones, which only add to the flavor.

To make this soup we have used shoulder of lamb, which is more readily available than the goat that is traditionally used. When the meat comes to the boil, carefully skim off any froth and bits of bone that float to the surface. Transfer the lamb into another pan and strain the stock. The cooking time in the spiced water depends on the quality of the meat: its juiciness, the time it's left to hang, the age of the animal, and so on. Also, don't use any salt when you start cooking because the meat will toughen.

The task of toasting the flour for the sauce requires some attention. Put it in a small heavy bottomed pan and keep it moving over a fairly brisk heat. This takes a while but it gradually turns light brown and gives off the smell of lightly toasted bread. As soon as it reaches this stage, whisk it with some stock from cooking the lamb until the sauce is smoothly blended and a golden brown color. It is then added to the soup and thickened with a lemon and egg mixture diluted with some hot stock so that all the ingredients are incorporated into the soup at the same temperature.

Wash the shoulder of lamb. Place it in a large pan filled with cold water. Bring to the boil then carefully remove any froth that forms on the surface.

Transfer the meat to another pan and add the cooking stock, passing it through a fine-mesh strainer. Add the cinnamon, nutmeg, cloves, allspice, peppercorns, and salt and leave to simmer for at least 1 hour.

Put the flour into a small heavy-bottomed pan and continue to stir it until it is lightly toasted. Dilute it with some stock from cooking the meat, whisking it all the time to ensure the sauce is thick and smooth.

Avgolemono Sauce

Continue to whisk the sauce while adding it to the pan with the lamb.

Put the eggs into a bowl and whisk with a hand-held electric beater. Add the lemon juice while whisking continuously.

Gradually add the cooking stock to the sauce until it starts to foam. Pour the sauce into the pan containing the lamb. Scatter with chopped mint and serve.

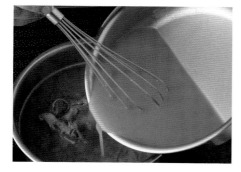

Chicken Soup

Preparation time: 35 minutes
Cooking time: 1 hour
40 minutes

Difficulty: ☆

Serves 4

1	free-range chicken weighing 4½ lb/ 2 kg (rooster, if possible)
1	onion
1	bay leaf

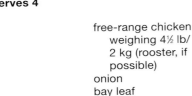

	black peppercorns
	salt
1 generous cup/ 125 g	rice
2	eggs
2	lemons
	black pepper

For the garnish (optional):
celery leaves

Chicken soup with *avgolemono* sauce is a classic in the Greek culinary repertoire. In Thessalia this dish is traditionally associated with Christmas. It is very filling and is often enjoyed as a main course.

Bursting with typically Greek flavors, the starring role goes to the rooster. This farmyard bird, eaten toward the end of its life, needs a long cooking time. Fans of this dish appreciate its firm flesh, although in some regions they use a boiling fowl instead, which tastes equally good.

This recipe only has a few ingredients but they are used wisely. The stock is flavored with peppercorns and onion and is enhanced with the special aroma of bay leaf. The evergreen bay tree grows wild in the Mediterranean. The leaves are used to give a lift to dishes that are simmered for a fairly long period of time, or are incorporated into mixes for fillings and marinades. After removing the chicken carcass, don't forget to strain the stock and reserve about 2–2½ cups/600 milliliters for the *avgolemono* sauce.

An ideal winter dish, this soup is very filling. The addition of the rice really makes this family dish special. Possibly originating in China, legend suggests that rice was imported to Mesopotamia by the Persians. After his expedition to India, Alexander the Great was keen to encourage the cultivation of rice in Macedonia. Regarded as a luxury in ancient times, today rice is eaten throughout the world.

Avgolemono sauce is found in a lot of Greek cooking, and really lends itself to this dish. It is always made from eggs, lemon juice, and stock, although cooks often add their own special touch. Panagiotis Delvenakiotis suggests adding a teaspoonful of cornstarch to help thicken and bind it.

Using a knife, make an incision in the chicken skin along the spine. Carefully remove the thighs. Cut the main carcass into 4 equal quarters and divide it, cutting the flesh away from the ribs, starting at the top of the breastbone. Discard the breastbone and remove the wings.

Put the chicken pieces into a large pan and add the whole peeled onion, the bay leaf and a few peppercorns. Cover with water. Put the lid on the pan and cook for 1½ hours, from time to time skimming off any froth that forms on the surface. Add salt to taste.

Remove the chicken pieces and reserve about 2–2½ cups/600 ml stock. Add the rice to the remaining stock and cook for about 10 minutes.

with Avgolemono

To make the sauce, separate the eggs and put the whites into a bowl while re-serving the yolks. Add some salt and whisk the egg whites until foaming.

Add the reserved egg yolks to the bowl and whisk.

Pour on the lemon juice. Whisk, and gradually add the reserved stock. Beat the sauce the whole time and add to the rice. Serve the soup in bowls sprinkled with black pepper and serve the meat separately. If desired, garnish both with celery leaves.

Navy Bean Soup

Preparation time:	25 minutes
Cooking time:	1 hour
	25 minutes
Soaking time (beans):	overnight
Difficulty:	★

Serves 4

2½ cups/500 g	dried white navy (haricot) beans
2	carrots
2 or 3 stalks	celery
2	onions
2	tomatoes
1 tbsp	tomato paste

	salt
	pepper
	olive oil
1 tsp	boukovo (flakes of dried red pimento)

To serve (optional):

chopped onion
smoked herring
black olives
red bell peppers

From time immemorial Greeks have come up with tasty recipes based on navy (haricot) beans, which they often serve with meat, vegetables, fish, and aromatic herbs. Navy bean soup, or *fasolada*, is always popular and can rightly be described as one of the country's "national dishes." Comforting and nourishing, it is ideal to serve hot in the winter.

Lots of different varieties of bean, or *fasola*, are grown throughout Greece. The ones that are most commonly used come from Kato Nevrokopi and are of medium size, either cylindrical or flat. A smaller bean is also grown in the Pelion region. Some people love to use the giant very soft beans grown around the Florina area to make this soup. All of them go well with tomato, onions, celery, and oregano.

Tomatoes will add a wonderful aroma and color to your soup. To peel them, use a sharp knife to score a little cross on their base. Plunge them into boiling water for about one minute, until the skin starts to loosen, then transfer to a bowl of iced water to refresh before peeling the skin. Tomatoes from the Cyclades, especially the ones grown on the islands of Syros and Santorini, have an excellent reputation, as have the ones from Nafplion and Argos in the Eastern Peloponnese and from Thessalonika in Macedonia.

The addition of *boukovo* to the soup is entirely optional. These yellow-orange colored flakes are obtained from small very spicy red pimentos that are dried then roughly processed in a special grinder.

This delicious dish, in which the refreshing taste of the olive oil counterbalances the fire of the pimentos, is good served with olives, pearl onions, and smoked herring. Don't forget to put a bottle of olive oil infused with herbs on the table so that each guest can add as much or as little as they want to the soup.

The night before you make the soup, soak the beans in a large pan filled with cold water. The next day, drain them and put into a pan filled with water. Bring to the boil then let the beans simmer briskly for about 15 minutes. Strain and cover again with clean water.

Meanwhile, prepare the other vegetables. Peel the carrots, cut off both ends, and slice into thin rounds. Cut the celery stalks into thin slices and finely chop the onions.

Peel the tomatoes as described above, cut them in half, and chop finely.

with Boukovo

Add the chopped onions, celery, and carrots to the saucepan containing the beans. Cook for 20 minutes.

Now add the fresh tomatoes and the tomato paste. Season and cook for another 30 minutes.

Finally add a trickle of olive oil and the boukovo, check the seasoning, and simmer gently for a further 20 minutes.

Garbanzo Bean Soup

Preparation time:	15 minutes
Cooking time:	1 hour
Soaking time (garbanzo beans):	overnight
Swelling time (garbanzo beans):	1 hour
Difficulty:	☆

Serves 6

2¼ lb/1 kg	garbanzo beans
2 tbsp/30 g	bicarbonate of soda

7 oz/200 g	onions
¾ cup/200 ml	olive oil
2 tbsp/30 g	all-purpose flour
2	lemons

For the garnish:

	dill sprigs

Garbanzo bean soup is an everyday Greek dish and is often accompanied by such side dishes as olives, sardines, and marinated vegetables known as *tursi* (eggplant, cauliflower, carrots, peppers, etc). Our chef has enriched his version with *delbia*, in which flour is mixed with lemon juice then diluted with stock. He uses this to thicken the soup and give it a sharper flavor. This is the same principle as *avgolemono*, which is made from lemon and beaten eggs, although *delbia* is primarily used for vegetable dishes when it is used to dress artichokes, cauliflower, fennel, spinach, and so on.

Nourishing and comforting, this soup is a wonderful illustration of the Greek imagination when it comes to vegetarian dishes. Obliged to observe a religious fast on half the days in the year, and living in an arid country where it was difficult to rear large numbers of animals, over the centuries they managed to develop delicious recipes based on vegetables and herbs. And the same is true today – dishes based on pulses are seldom enriched with meat.

When you are cooking the garbanzo beans in boiling water, make sure that from time to time you skim off the froth from the surface. Leave the beans in the water until they are half cooked then mash them lightly. You can then add the sautéed onions. The olive oil is only added at the end of the cooking time, when it lends its fresh aroma to the soup.

To serve, garnish the soup with a sprig of dill or fennel (use one that has a strong scent of aniseed), but don't cook either the dill or the fennel with the soup itself. Just add the herb as a garnish so that its full flavor is retained.

If you have any of the soup left over, like the Greeks you can always make another meal out of it by adding some boiled rice.

Leave the garbanzo beans to soak overnight in a large pan of cold water. Drain them, put into a dish and sprinkle with bicarbonate of soda. Leave the garbanzo beans to swell for about 1 hour.

Put the garbanzo beans into a towel and rub them to remove the skins. Rinse in cold water and put them into a large pan filled with water, bring to the boil and cook for 30 minutes.

Peel and chop the onions. Add them to the garbanzo beans and cook for another 30 minutes.

with Delbia

When the garbanzo beans are tender, add a dash of olive oil.

In a small bowl, whisk the flour with the lemon juice. Continue whisking while at the same time adding a little stock from cooking the garbanzo beans.

Incorporate the flour and lemon sauce into the garbanzo beans and stir briskly over the heat. Serve the soup piping hot garnished with a sprig of dill and a dash of olive oil.

Mani-style

Preparation time: 40 minutes
Cooking time: 35 minutes
Difficulty: ✷

Serves 4

3½ lb/1.5 kg	pollock (or cod)
1	carrot
1 stalk	celery
1	onion
⅔ cup/150 ml	olive oil
7 oz/200 g	pearl onions

1 lb 2 oz/500 g	tomatoes
⅔ cup 150 ml	white wine
	salt
	pepper
9 oz/250 g	potatoes

To serve (optional):
croutons

For the garnish:
celery leaves

In Greece, the sea is never very far away. On this land blessed by the gods, Poseidon generously offered all the treasures of his watery kingdom to the inhabitants – fish, shellfish, crustaceans. The cluster of tiny villages in the Mani region pays regular homage to this mythological deity through their cuisine.

Famous throughout the country, Mani-style fish soup is traditionally eaten in winter. Easy to make, this specialty from the coast stars pollock as its main ingredient. Greatly appreciated for its firm white flesh and pleasant consistency, it is often found at fishmongers cut into fillets or steaks. If it is hard to obtain pollock, cod can be used instead. Around the islands of the Aegean Sea, local fishermen sometimes use grouper fish or hake for this dish.

In this recipe, products from the soil also play an important role. Olive oil, also produced in the Mani region, is used to

flavor the pearl onions. Pearl onions, which originally came from Asia, have been cultivated for more than 5,000 years. The flavor of the ones grown around the Mediterranean is particularly subtle.

This dish allows the characteristic taste of celery to shine through. Available all year round on market stalls, this vegetable is esteemed for its fresh flavor and crunchy texture. Used for soups, stews, and sauces, it grows wild in Greece, where it is known as *selino*. Celery is a rich source of sodium chloride. The heads should be bright green, have no blemishes, no signs of wilting, and no yellowing at the base of the stalks. To keep them fresh, stand the base of the celery stalk in cold salted water.

This delicious fish dish is usually served with croutons. Greek families usually serve the fish and the soup separately at the table.

Use a sharp knife to make an incision into the pollock following the line of the dorsal fin to fillet it. Cut the fish into thick slices and remove the skin. Clean off the fish bones and put to one side.

In a large pan of water, make a stock from the prepared carrot, celery, and onion. Add the cleaned fish bones. Let the stock cook for 20 minutes, skimming off any froth that forms.

Heat the olive oil in a separate pan and add the peeled pearl onions. Peel and chop the tomatoes into small pieces, add to the pan and cook for about 5 minutes.

Fish Soup

Add the white wine, cook for about 5 minutes, and season to taste. Peel the potatoes and, using a melon baller, cut the potatoes into little balls.

Strain the stock and pour half onto the onion and tomato mixture. Cook the potatoes in the rest of the stock.

Lay the slices of pollock on top of the onion mixture and cook for 4 minutes. Serve the strained soup with the croutons (if using) in one bowl, and the fish on another plate with the potatoes and pearl onions. Garnish with celery leaves.

Mount Athos

Preparation time: 40 minutes
Cooking time: 40 minutes
Difficulty: ☆

Serves 4

5	pearl onions
10 oz/300 g	potatoes
3 oz/80 g	carrots
1 oz/30 g	red radish
1 lb 2 oz/500 g	grouper fish fillets
	salt
	pepper
	olive oil
½	lemon

For the fish stock:

1	carrot
1	onion
1 stalk	celery
7 oz/200 g	fish trimmings (head, skin, fins)
1	bay leaf
1 sprig	thyme

For the garnish:

	bay leaf
	parsley
	dill

An area of outstanding beauty, Mount Athos on the tip of the Macedonian peninsula is a unique part of Greece. Devoted exclusively to spiritual meditation, only men were allowed to live there, and it has been inhabited by monks since the middle of the 11th century. Governed by extremely strict rules that border on asceticism, the monks have developed an original culinary repertoire through the ages. Seafood plays a major role in their diet, and these days the cuisine of the many monasteries that abound in this area is famous throughout the country.

This fish soup is a typical Mount Athos dish, which is usually made on a day commemorating a saint. Easy to make, the delicate taste of the grouper fish is enhanced by the other ingredients. Popular for its white, very dense flesh, the taste is nonetheless light. A medium sized fish, it is available all year round from fishmongers.

An impregnable fortress, Mount Athos seems protected by the crystalline waters of the Aegean Sea. According to tradition, only the monks are permitted to fish there. Being completely self-sufficient, they are also skilled gardeners. Scrupulously following the rhythm of the seasons, they use the produce from their vegetable gardens to good effect.

Grown in China for more than 3,000 years, radishes were already regarded as a delicacy by the Ancient Greeks. Easy to grow, this edible root vegetable is eaten raw, lightly dipped in salt. A member of the same family as the turnip, which can be used instead of radish in this recipe, market stalls are heaped with these pretty vegetables in March. Choose firm ones with fresh, crisp leaves and no blemishes.

This delicious soup marvelously illustrates the simplicity of monastic cuisine.

For the fish stock, peel the carrot, onion, and celery and roughly chop them.

Heat 4 cups/1 l water in a large pan. Add the fish trimmings, celery, carrot, onion, bay leaf, and thyme. Cook for about 20 minutes, skimming off any froth that forms on the top.

Pass the stock through a fine-mesh strainer twice, and reserve.

Fish Soup

Peel the pearl onions, potatoes, and carrots. Finely peel the radish with a knife. Carve the carrots into a pointed shape.

Reheat the reserved stock, add the vegetables, and cook for about 10 minutes. Season the fillets of grouper fish. Add the fish to the pan with a dash of olive oil. Cook for about 5 minutes.

Add the juice of half a lemon to the mixture and cook for 5 minutes. Check the seasoning. Serve the soup in shallow bowls each garnished with a bay leaf, chopped parsley and dill.

Yalitiki

Preparation time:	20 minutes
Cooking time:	50 minutes
Difficulty:	✭

Serves 4

2¼ lb/1 kg	shin of beef, boned and rolled
	salt
4	carrots
1 head	celery
	peppercorns

| 2¼ lbs/1 kg | onions |
| 3½ tbsp | olive oil |

A Venetian fortress has dominated the large harbor at Sitia on the easternmost coast of Crete for several centuries. The Serene Republic, which conquered and governed Crete from 1211 to 1660, also left a number of influences on the local cuisine. This soup of boiled beef prepared by our chef comes into that category. In Greek, it is known as *yalitiki*.

George Anastassakis is anxious to reintroduce this recipe, which he believes is on the brink of disappearing from the Greek culinary repertoire. In the 1970s, when mass tourism was developing in Crete, some cooks were willing to mix carelessly different European styles of cooking. These days, however, traditional dishes are coming back into fashion, and are very much appreciated by tourists anxious to discover original Greek culinary traditions.

When making this dish, our chef normally uses *moschari*, meat from an older calf (or young bullock) in which the flesh is already red. It is easy to replace this with ordinary beef, which is the nearest to it in terms of texture and appearance. Knuckle of veal (*kotsi* in Greece) is the best cut of meat to use for this dish because it contains gelatin, which helps to thicken the soup.

Please note that the stalks of celery are only used to add flavor to the stock and are not eaten as part of the meal itself. Celery can be easily substituted with celeriac that is cut into cubes.

It is up to you whether you want to add the onions raw directly to the beef stock when it is three-quarters cooked. However, as these will be served with the meat, it is better to brown them in a frying pan before adding them to the soup. Also, the flavor of fried onions really enhances the aroma of the stock.

Cut the shin of beef into thick slices of just under 1 in/2 cm.

The slices then need to be trussed. Wrap a piece of cooking string around the outside of each piece of meat, tie it with a knot, and trim off the loose ends.

Put the pieces of meat into a large pan. Fill with water and add salt to taste. Bring to the boil and leave to cook for about 10 minutes.

Soup

If too much froth forms on the surface, skim it off using a slotted spoon.

Peel the carrots, trim the celery stalks, reserving some leaves, and add the stalks and some leaves to the pan with the peppercorns. Continue cooking for about 30 minutes.

Chop the onions and fry in a skillet with a little olive oil. Add them to the pan and cook for a further 10 minutes. Lift out the meat, remove the string, and discard the celery. Ladle the broth into the serving bowls, add the beef, vegetables, and a few celery leaves.

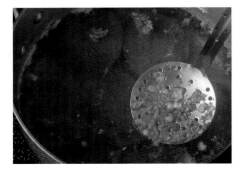

Trachanosoupa

Preparation time:	15 minutes
Cooking time:	35 minutes
Difficulty:	✶

Serves 4

7 oz/250 g	small tomatoes
4 tbsp/60 ml	olive oil
5½ oz/150 g	trachana (roughly pounded grains of wheat)
4	eggs
	salt

4 slices	goat milk cheese
1 scant cup/ 100 g	all-purpose flour
3 tbsp	vegetable oil

Greek families usually eat this traditional soup in winter. It is made from *trachana* (grains of roughly pounded sun-dried wheat), tomato, eggs, and cheese. Easy to make, this extremely popular dish is often served as a main course.

Wheat has been cultivated in Greece for thousands of years. It is an annual cereal, a member of the graminaceous family, the grains used to produce flour and semolina. Highly prized in Ancient Greece, it was used to make flat breads and other types of bread.

Typically Greek, *trachana* can also be turned into a type of pasta. Still made in local villages, the grains of wheat are sometimes soaked in milk before they are dried under the sun on a large cloth. They are used in certain specialties of the country, particularly soups, their slightly sharp taste adding something special. If you can't find it, use bulgur wheat instead.

This national specialty also stars tomatoes. On the Island of Chios, where our chef comes from, the tomatoes are particularly small. Grown primarily in the south of the island on non-irrigated soil, they decorate village balconies during the winter months. When dried they become quite hard and firm.

Brought back from Peru by the Spanish Conquistadors, tomatoes today feature in much Mediterranean cookery. A vegetable that revels in the sun, they can be found in abundance at every market throughout Greece in the summer. For this recipe, try to use the Roma variety, which is very tasty. Choose well-ripened tomatoes that are plump, shiny, and have a uniform color.

The goat milk cheese meanwhile, another favorite ingredient in Greece, adds its own characteristic flavor to this dish and gives the *trachanasoupa* a real lift.

Plunge the tomatoes into boiling water for about 1 minute until the skins loosen. Refresh in ice water. Peel, then pass them through a mouli, or quickly blend, to form a purée.

Pour 4 cups/1 l water into a large pan, add the puréed tomatoes, and blend using a whisk. Add 4 tbsp olive oil. Cook for about 15 minutes.

Add the trachana. Gently mix and cook for about 5 minutes.

Break the eggs into the cooking pan. Let them cook for about 3 minutes. Season with a little salt.

Remove some of the salt from the goat milk cheese by putting the slices into very cold water for a few minutes. Drain and pat dry with paper towels. Coat the slices with flour. Heat the vegetable oil in a skillet and fry the cheese.

Pour the soup into small ovenproof dishes. Top each one with slices of cheese. Cook in an oven preheated to 475° F/ 240° C for 1 minute. Take the trachanosoupa to the table and serve.

Vegetable
Dishes

Eggplant with

Preparation time:	20 minutes
Cooking time:	45 minutes
Difficulty:	⭐

Serves 4

7 oz/200 g	yellow split peas
7 oz/200 g	onions
1	carrot
	salt
	pepper
1 tsp	sugar

⅔ cup/150 ml	olive oil
½ tsp	dried oregano
2	medium eggplants
7 oz/200 g	tomatoes
8	dried tomatoes
2 tsp	capers

For the garnish:

	olive oil

Greek cookery is famous throughout the world for the wonderful use it makes of vegetables. The inhabitants of this Mediterranean country love vegetarian dishes and throughout the centuries they have paid homage to Demeter, goddess of the bountiful harvest.

Typical of the islands dotted around the Aegean Sea, eggplant with fava purée can be enjoyed as either a hot appetizer or as a main course. This delicious traditional recipe is easy to make and combines fresh and dried vegetables with great flair.

In Greek the word *fava* is the generic word for beans and split peas. Found in abundance on market stalls, split peas are often reduced to a purée, as is the case in our recipe. Usually cooked with onions and seasoned with lemon juice, they also make a flavorsome appearance as a *mezze* when Greeks take their aperitif.

A wonderful source of energy, yellow split peas are rich in phosphorus and potassium. They start life as the seed of the pea, and are picked in summer when they are fully ripe. After their cellulose outer cover has been removed, they take on their distinctive semispherical shape. An essential ingredient in Aegean cooking, these little dried legumes have the additional advantage of being able to be cooked in many different ways and incorporated with a wide variety of ingredients. On the island of Santorini, for example, they are shaped into little balls and served with cod.

These days split peas are often used with eggplants. A superb summer vegetable, eggplants originally came from India. Prized for their distinctive flavor, they take center stage in many Greek and Mediterranean specialties. Grown primarily in the Arcadia region of Greece, the *Tsakonikes* eggplant variety had established a name for itself as long ago as the Byzantine Age.

Put the yellow split peas into a large pan filled with water. Heat, and when the water is boiling skim off any froth that forms on the surface.

Add 1 peeled and chopped onion and carrot to the split peas and cook for between 40 and 45 minutes. Season, and add the sugar and a dash of olive oil. Stir in the oregano, and strain and purée if necessary. Set the mix to one side.

Peel the eggplants lengthwise in strips, to achieve a striped appearance, and cut into big chunks. Heat 3–4 tbsp olive oil in a skillet and brown the eggplant. Remove and blot with paper towels.

Fava Purée

Peel and finely chop the remaining onions. Wash and roughly chop the fresh tomatoes. Chop the dried tomatoes.

Heat the remaining olive oil in a pan and add the onions. Cover with water and simmer gently for about 15 minutes. Add the fresh and dried tomatoes. Cook for a further 10 minutes, then add the capers. Season and cook for another 5 minutes.

Put the eggplant into an ovenproof dish and cover with half the tomato sauce. Cook in an oven preheated to 350° F/ 180° C for 20 minutes. Divide the rest of the sauce between the 4 serving plates, put the eggplant on top and spoon the fava purée around. Drizzle with olive oil.

Chortomageria

Preparation time:	*20 minutes*
Cooking time:	*40 minutes*
Soaking time	
(black-eyed peas):	*2 hours*
Difficulty:	✶

Serves 4

3½ oz/100 g	black-eyed peas
8 oz/225 g	leeks
2	zucchini
8 oz/225 g	Swiss chard
8 oz/225 g	spinach

1 bunch	flat-leaf parsley
1 bunch	mint
5½ oz/150 g	button mushrooms
5 or 6	red onions
½ cup/125 ml	olive oil
1	large potato
	salt
	pepper

For thousands of years Greeks have been blessed with a vast range of wild and cultivated plants that thrive in the country's special microclimate. They make use of these in two ways – either in salads or made into a main course. In the first case they are washed in plenty of water, then drained and dressed with olive oil and lemon. In the second, they are cooked either on their own or with meat, dried pulses, snails, cheese, grapes, etc. They are also used as pie fillings. The variety of plants is so great that even the same recipe differs between one region and another.

Eaten as a main course, *chortomageria* is quick to make. A dish that is simmered with herbs, it tastes best when made from a range of wild aromatic plants. But like our chef, you can replace these with a mix of leeks, spinach, Swiss chard, mint, and parsley, with equally good results. You could also add some button mushrooms or ceps.

Make sure you have a really big pan available to cook all of these vegetables, which will take up a lot of room when you first put them in. While it is cooking over the heat make sure you stir up everything from the bottom of the pan so that it all cooks uniformly, then put the lid on and let it simmer. Next time you look you'll find the volume of vegetables has reduced considerably!

The *chortomageria* is enriched with black-eyed peas that turn it into a filling vegetarian dish. These small beige-colored pulses with their little black circles are close cousins of navy (haricot) beans. The Greeks call them *mavromatica fasolia* or *gifto fasolia* (giant haricot beans).

As with all cooked vegetarian dishes, *chortomageria* is usually served with cubes of feta cheese. Serve hot, or even warm in summer.

Wash the black-eyed peas. Leave them to soak for two hours in water then boil for 15 minutes. Drain and set aside.

Wash the leeks and zucchini and cut them into fat slices. Wash and roughly chop the Swiss chard, spinach, parsley, and mint, keeping a few whole mint leaves for decoration. Wipe the mushrooms and cut in half. Mix everything together.

Peel and roughly chop the onions. Heat the oil in a large pan and fry the onions.

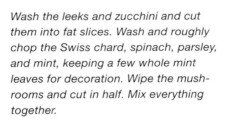

When the onions start to soften add the mixture of herbs, vegetables, and mushrooms. Cover and cook for about 5 minutes.

Peel the potato, cut into cubes, and add to the pan. Add a dash of oil and leave to cook for another 10 minutes.

Add the black-eyed peas. Season to taste and add a little water. Cook over a gentle heat until the liquid starts to reduce then serve hot, garnished with mint.

Stuffed Zucchini with

Preparation time:	40 minutes	
Cooking time:	1 hour	
	5 minutes	
Difficulty:	★★	

Serves 6

12	medium zucchini
3	onions
9 oz/250 g	rice
2 tbsp	chopped flat-leaf parsley
1 tbsp	chopped mint
	olive oil

	salt
	pepper
1	carrot
1 head	celery
1 sprig	dill
3	chicken drumsticks
2	eggs
1	lemon

Zucchini filled with rice is a very popular summer dish throughout the whole of Greece. In former times, Greek cooks used to fill them with any ingredients they happened to have to hand (vegetables, meat, spices…) and thus delicious recipes were developed. Anastasios Tolis has chosen to coat them with *avgolemono* in this recipe, a sauce based on lemon and eggs.

Just like the tomatoes and potatoes that these days so deliciously enrich many Greek dishes, zucchini too made only a late appearance in the country's cuisine. Thousands of years ago the diet of the Indians of Central America included many different varieties of squash, which were later brought to Europe by the Spanish Conquistadors. In the 18th century, some Italian gourmands had the idea of eating them before they were fully grown, and these were the forerunners of what we know today as zucchini, which means "little squash" in Italian. The Greeks call them

kolokythakia, and they traditionally eat both the flesh and the flowers, either filled, fried, or *au gratin*, i.e. cooked with breadcrumbs and topped with cheese.

The vegetables in this dish are filled with a delicious mixture of rice flavored with onions, parsley, and mint. Our chef prefers to use long grain white Carolina rice, although you can use your own favorite kind. The mixture inside the zucchini is cooked in the water or the stock in which the chicken drumsticks are cooked. The stuffing can also be used to fill bell peppers, tomatoes, or eggplant.

A few bones from a freshly bought chicken or some drumsticks will add greatly to the flavor of the juice from cooking the zucchini. This will then be used hot to dilute the egg and lemon mixture. Everything is vigorously whisked together and the resulting smooth, blended sauce is gently reheated then poured over the zucchini.

Cut a little piece off each end of the zucchini to make a "hat." Using a potato peeler or a melon baller, carefully scoop out the flesh, which should then be chopped. Peel and chop the onions.

Mix the rice with the parsley and mint. Heat some oil in a skillet and fry two-thirds of the chopped onions. Add the rice and herbs and mix well. Add the zucchini flesh and just enough water to cover. Season to taste and cook at a rolling boil for 15 minutes.

When the stuffing mixture is thoroughly cooked, spoon it inside the zucchini.

Avgolemono Sauce

Peel and slice the carrot, trim the celery. Place in a heavy-bottomed pan, together with the dill, remaining chopped onion, and the chicken drumsticks.

Lay the stuffed zucchini on the bed of vegetables and chicken. Add some water, cover and steam over medium heat for 30–40 minutes.

Meanwhile, put the eggs and the lemon juice into a bowl. Whisk them together, gradually adding a little hot stock from cooking the zucchini. When the zucchini are ready, arrange on a serving dish, coat with the sauce, and garnish with dill.

Trachanas, Onion, and Mint

Preparation time: 40 minutes
Cooking time: 1 hour
5 minutes
Resting time (pastry): 30 minutes
Difficulty: ★★

Serves 6

For the phyllo (filo) pastry:
2⅔ cups/300 g	all-purpose flour
1 tsp	salt
1 tsp	bicarbonate of soda
2 cups/500 ml	very cold water
1 cup/250 ml	olive oil
1	egg

For the filling:
1¾ cups/400 ml	milk
3½ oz/100 g	trachanas
1 lb 5 oz/600 g	shallots
3 tbsp	olive oil
4	eggs
7 oz/200 g	feta
1 bunch	fresh mint
	salt
	pepper

This recipe for *trachanas*, onion, and mint pie made with phyllo (filo) pastry comes from the ancient city of Thebes. It represents an interesting blend of ingredients that typify Greek cuisine: onions, mint, *trachanas*, and olive oil.

Greeks have been cooking with phyllo pastry for thousands of years. The first reference dates right back to the 3rd century B.C. in Macedonia. Inventive pie-makers found a way of replacing heavy yeast-based pizza-type pastry with a light flaky pastry made with lard.

This type of pastry is known throughout Greece as *phyllo*, the Greek word for leaf. The word accurately describes the action of rolling out the pastry into tissue-thin sheets. If the mix is too soft, don't hesitate to add a bit of flour. Always leave it to rest for a while so that everything blends smoothly. This also makes it easier to roll.

Trachanas are very small dried, yellowish colored pulses that add both flavor and texture to the pie filling. They are based on a mixture of crushed wheat or flour, salt, and either goat's milk or ewe's milk, which is then kneaded, crumbled, and dried for one week. There are two sorts available: *xinos trachanas* (bitter, made with sour milk) and *glykos trachanas* (sweet). They keep for a long time and are widely used in phyllo pastry pies and soups.

The pie filling is subtly flavored with the fresh taste of mint, but basil could replace the mint.

Our chef decorates his pie with little shavings of fried carrots, tomato, and mint. He suggests you do as the Greeks do and serve it with a bowl of natural Greek yogurt.

To make the pastry, put the flour, salt and bicarbonate of soda into a bowl, make a well, and gradually add the water and ¾ cup/200 ml of the olive oil. Add 1 egg. Knead the dough well and leave it to rest for 30 minutes.

Sprinkle your work surface with flour. Divide the pastry into 6 balls and sprinkle them with flour. Roll each one out until you end up with 6 tissue-thin sheets of pastry. Cover with a damp cloth.

To make the filling, pour the milk into a pan and bring it to the boil. Stir in the trachanas and cook for about 5 minutes.

Pie made with Phyllo Pastry

Peel and finely chop the shallots. Heat the olive oil in a skillet and fry the shallots. Stir the fried shallots into the cooked trachanas.

Whisk the eggs in a bowl then add cubes of feta, chopped mint, and season with salt and pepper. Pour the contents of the bowl into the trachanas and stir everything together over the heat for another 5 minutes.

Line the bottom of a greased ovenproof dish with 3 sheets of phyllo, ensuring the edges of the pastry hang over the side of the dish. Add the filling and cover with the 3 remaining sheets of pastry, sealing the edge firmly. Bake in an oven preheated to 350° F/180° C for 50 minutes.

Okra in

Preparation time: 10 minutes
Cooking time: 20 minutes
Difficulty: *

Serves 4

1½ lb/600 g	okra
	salt
4 tbsp	wine vinegar
5½ oz/150 g	onions
7 oz/200 g	tomatoes
scant ½ cup/ 100 ml	olive oil

	pepper
1 bunch	parsley

For the garnish:

chives (optional)
olive oil

Devotees of vegetarian dishes since olden times, Greeks have always shown a great talent for coming up with wonderful ways of cooking them. In their culinary repertoire, vegetables play an important role in many original dishes.

Okra in olive oil is a favorite throughout Greece. Easy to make, this springtime recipe can be served hot or warm.

Grown primarily in Pilea on the outskirts of Thessalonika, okra from this area has been rewarded with the accolade of *appellation d'origine contrôlée*. Known as *bamies* in Greek, they are also known as *okra*, which literally translated means "lady's finger."

Now grown extensively across the Mediterranean and in the West Indies, these vegetables probably originated from Africa. According to our chef they were introduced into the northeast region of Greece by merchants and travelers in previous centuries. Available in specialist delicatessens, the best okra should measure less than 4 inches/10 centimeters long and be a pretty green color. Before blanching them, be careful to clean them with a cloth and to remove the rough hairy coating. Nicolaos Katsanis adds his own personal refinement to the dish by serving them in a bundle, using a stem of chives to hold them together.

Carefully flavored with olive oil, another star ingredient in this recipe, okra is sometimes enriched with chicken, beef, or even grouper fish. In this case, just cook the *bamies* at the same time as the tomatoes. Add the meat or fish immediately and leave it all to simmer for 25 minutes.

We suggest that you discover the delights of this dish with a glass of white *retsina*, one of the most popular wines in Greece.

Using a sharp knife, cut off the conical ends of the okra.

Bring a pan of salted water to the boil and add the okra and the wine vinegar. Cook for about 5 minutes.

Lift out the okra in a small sieve so the cooking liquid can drain off and transfer them to a bowl filled with clean water and about 10 ice cubes. Leave them to cool for 5 minutes, then drain.

Olive Oil

Peel and finely dice the onions and blanch, peel and finely chop the tomatoes.

Pour the diced onions into the olive oil and add the tomatoes. Stir well with a flat wooden spoon.

Add the okra to the tomato mixture. Cook for 10 minutes. Season, and scatter with chopped parsley. Partially cover and cook for 5 minutes. Divide the okra into 4 servings, stand a bundle of okra on each plate and tie it with a stem of chives. Add sauce, and drizzle with olive oil.

Didymo

Preparation time:	20 minutes		12	eggs
Cooking time:	15 minutes			pepper
Difficulty:	★			salt (optional)
			4 oz/115 g	black olives, pitted
Serves 4			1 tsp	dried oregano

1 lb/450 g	tomatoes
2	onions
10 oz/300 g	potatoes
	vegetable oil for frying
4 tbsp	olive oil
7 oz/200 g	*touloumi* (goat milk cheese) or feta

In the Greek culinary repertoire, the word *kayanas* means "solid omelet." Originally eaten by people in the country-side, this dish is an opportunity of marrying eggs with a whole range of different ingredients. Depending on what's available in the market, or just on the mood of the moment, you can allow your imagination free rein with this one.

In Didymo in the Peloponnese, this traditional recipe is particularly popular, magnifying as it does the typically Greek flavors. It only uses produce from the land.

Simplicity itself to make, the *kayanas* can be enjoyed as a hot appetizer or as a main course. Ideal for an improvized meal, this vegetarian dish is extremely tasty.

Similar to an Italian *frittata*, this omelet uses fried pota-toes. Legend tells how the Greeks discovered potatoes thanks to the ingeniousness of Kapodistria, head of the provisional government. Exiled in Switzerland by the Ottoman authorities, when he returned to Greece, Kapodistria brought some seedlings with him.

To reduce the scorn of his contemporaries for this new veg-etable, he had the idea of planting them in public gardens. Guards were employed to keep a watch over them as they grew. But in reaction to this, the people dug up the precious plants and replanted them across the whole of Greece! These days the islands of Naxos and Paros in the Aegean Sea specialize in growing potatoes.

Extremely hearty and warming, it is as if the rays of the sun were concentrated in this dish and the addition of the black olives is a reminder of its geographical origins. Greeks adore olives and more than a thousand varieties grow in the country. Our chef suggests using Kalamata olives, which have a particularly good reputation in his country.

Wash the tomatoes. Peel the onions. Using a sharp knife cut both vegetables into small dice.

Carefully scrub any soil off the skins of the potatoes, wipe dry, and cut into thin wedges. Heat some vegetable oil in a skillet and fry the potatoes. Blot dry on paper towels.

Heat the olive oil in a pan and fry first the diced onions, then add the tomatoes, and cook for about 5 minutes.

Kayanas

Add cubes of cheese to the mixture and stir. Break the eggs into a bowl and season with pepper. Add salt to taste, if desired.

Add the pitted black olives and the oregano to the eggs, then the potato wedges, and gently mix.

Add the egg mixture to the tomato, onion, and cheese mixture. Cook for about 4 minutes, or until firm. Cut the Didymo kayanas into 4 and serve.

Chiropoiita Macaroni

Preparation time:	50 minutes			3	fresh white onions
Cooking time:	15 minutes			2 sprigs	dill
Soaking time				3½ oz/100 g	baby zucchini
(garbanzo beans):	12 hours			2¼ lb/1 kg	tomatoes
Resting time (pasta):	15 minutes			5 tbsp	olive oil
Drying time (macaronia):	2–8 hours				salt
Difficulty:	★★				pepper (optional)

Serves 4

2 oz/55 g	goat milk cheese
	(finely grated)

For the sauce:

¾ cup/85 g	garbanzo beans
1 tsp	bicarbonate of soda

For the pasta:

9 oz/250 g	all-purpose flour,
	sifted (or pasta flour)
3 tbsp	olive oil

For the garnish:

	dill

In the northeast Aegean, there is a trio of extraordinary islands, Lesbos, Samos, and Chios (where our chef comes from). Each has its own individual cultural, historic, and gastronomic charms. Typical of the little villages in the southern part of Chios, our *macaronia chiropoiita*, served here with tomato sauce, is made from garbanzo beans and fresh vegetables. Reasonably easy to make, this festive vegetarian dish is full of unforgettable flavors.

Still made by local families, *macaronia chiropoiita* takes its name from the Greek *chiro*, or "hand," and *poiita*, which comes from the verb *poio*, "to create." The pasta dough, which is made into long tubes, is usually shaped around twigs from a bush called *sparto* which grows naturally on Chios. You can easily substitute the *sparto* with long toothpicks. Don't forget to leave the *macaronia* to rest before plunging it into the boiling water. The Greeks usually put them into a cloth and leave them out in the sun to dry for

two hours before cooking them. You could also leave them under artificial light for about eight hours.

This traditional recipe is very filling thanks to the addition of the garbanzo beans. These originated in the Mediterranean basin, but later became widespread in this part of the world thanks to Phoenician traders. Homer, who it seems was born on Chios, even mentions them in *The Iliad*.

These days they are primarily grown on the island of Sifnos in the Aegean Sea. Garbanzo beans are the seeds of an annual herbaceous plant. Recognizable by their cream color, they are highly prized for their underlying taste of hazelnut. In accordance with the culinary customs of the Greek Orthodox Church, they are associated with the many days and periods on which the faithful are prohibited from consuming either meat or fish, and they also play an important role in monastic cuisine.

Fill a bowl with water and let the garbanzo beans soak for 12 hours. Drain but reserve the water. Sprinkle the garbanzo beans with bicarbonate of soda. Leave for 5 minutes, then cook them in the soaking water for 20 minutes, then drain.

Peel and finely chop the onions, together with the dill. Dice the washed, but unpeeled, zucchini. Chop the tomatoes and reduce down to a purée by cooking in 2 tbsp of olive oil for about 5 minutes. Season to taste and set the purée to one side.

Heat the remaining olive oil in a skillet and fry the onions. Add the zucchini, garbanzo beans, and dill. Season with salt to taste and cook for 5 minutes.

with Tomato Sauce

To make the macaronia (pasta), put the flour into a bowl and pour over the olive oil. Work them together adding about 1¼ cups/300 ml water a few drops at a time. Knead until a pliable dough is obtained. Leave to rest for 15 minutes.

Sprinkle some flour on the work surface. Roll strips of dough into a long cigarette shape then cut it into little cubes. Holding these in the palm of the hand, roll them around a toothpick to create the macaronia, then slide out the toothpick. Leave to dry for 2–8 hours.

Put the macaronia into a pan of salted boiling water and boil for 5 minutes. Drain well and add to the garbanzo bean mixture. Stir well. Serve the pasta topped with the tomato sauce and scattered with finely grated goat milk cheese. Garnish with dill.

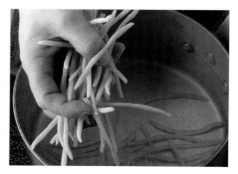

Leeks with

Preparation time:	20 minutes
Cooking time:	25 minutes
Difficulty:	★

Serves 4

1	red onion
6	medium leeks
5–6 tbsp	olive oil
¾ cup/200 ml	tomato juice
1 pinch	nutmeg

	salt
	pepper
9 oz/250 g	pitted prunes

The inhabitants of Yannina, the capital of the mountainous region of Epirus, have developed a vegetarian recipe that mixes leeks, tomato sauce, onions, and prunes. In Greece, the Orthodox Church prescribes 145 days of fasting every year, particularly before Easter and Christmas. Ordinary fasting prohibits the faithful from consuming meat and any animal produce (milk, eggs, cheese, etc). Complete fasting (observed during grand ceremonies), strictly limits the meal to virtually nothing but vegetables, fruit, and bread. The Greeks have invented delicious recipes for these times. They have managed to make subtle allies of sweet and bitter and sweet and salty.

Up until the 1970s no Greek family dared eat any of the prohibited products on one of these fasting days. There then followed a period when Greek vegetarian dishes were shunned in favor of more "international" cuisine, but the traditional vegetarian dishes are now back in fashion.

When served as the main course, leeks with Yannina prunes are usually accompanied by salads and olives.

A small hop away from central Greece, we find the island of Skopelos, part of the northern Sporades in the Thessalia region. Most of the prunes eaten in Greece over the past centuries have come from this part of the country. They are prepared from plums that contain a lot of sugar, are oblong in shape, and of medium size. Their skins are smooth and their flesh is a violet-brown. Harvested in August, the fruit is first spread out and dried for 10–15 days on a bed of straw, heather, or on top of a fine mesh grid. They are then put into a cool oven overnight to dry.

When the leeks and prunes have finished cooking, our chef recommends that you wait a while until you serve them. Cover and leave to rest for several minutes so that the flavors have a chance to develop and complement one another.

Peel and finely chop the onion. Wash the white part of the leeks and cut into 2-in/5-cm slices.

Heat the oil in a heavy-bottomed pan. Add the leeks and leave to brown, turning them so they end up a uniform color.

Add the chopped onion and stir over the heat until it is also thoroughly browned.

Yannina Prunes

Pour the tomato juice over the vegetables and bring to the boil.

Add the grated nutmeg, and season to taste with salt and pepper. Cook for 5 minutes over a gentle heat.

Finally add the prunes. Cover and finish cooking for 5 minutes. Remove from the heat, put a lid on the pan and leave to rest for several minutes before serving.

Stuffed Tomatoes and

Preparation time: 30 minutes
Cooking time: 1 hour
25 minutes
Difficulty: ★★

Serves 6

6	very ripe tomatoes
6	large green bell peppers
1 cup/100 g	pine nuts
¾ cup/100 g	chopped almonds
1	onion
1 cup/250 ml	extra-virgin olive oil

½ cup/100 g	rice
1 cup/125 g	golden raisins
2 cloves	garlic
3½ oz/100 g	scallions
1 tsp	ground cinnamon
1 cup/250 ml	tomato juice
¾ oz/20 g	fresh mint
	salt
	freshly ground black pepper
1 tbsp	sugar
1 oz/30 g	flat-leaf parsley

Tomatoes and peppers stuffed with rice, pine nuts, almonds, golden raisins, and herbs are one of the specialties of the island of Samos. Situated in the eastern Aegean, just a few nautical miles from Turkey, this island still retains a tradition of the sweet-salted dishes that are typical of Asia Minor. The Greeks love fresh stuffed vegetables: They eat tomatoes, bell peppers, eggplants, zucchini, or potatoes filled with rice and herbs during meat-free religious days, and incorporate finely chopped meat the rest of the year.

To prepare the vegetables, first slice a bit off the base so that they will stand upright in the cooking dish, then cut off a little "lid." Our chef suggests you use the following method for hollowing out the tomato: Stick the tip of the knife half-way up and slice around the tomato so that you cut the flesh inside it at the same time. Use a melon baller to scoop out the flesh.

The amount of rice you will need for the stuffing depends on the size of the tomatoes and bell peppers. Try to use fine white rice that doesn't swell too much during cooking. It will only need to be half cooked in the tomato sauce as it will continue cooking inside the vegetables.

In their version of this dish the inhabitants of Samos use *samiotiko*, locally grown tiny pale yellow grapes dried into golden raisins. Samos has 5,685 acres/2,300 hectares of vines planted in terraces. Local vine growers produce grapes for one of the most famous dessert wines in the world, Samos Muscat, with its mellow, refreshing, flavor.

The sugary taste of the stuffing comes from the dried fruits. However, don't hesitate to smear a little powdered sugar around the inside of the vegetables. During the cooking time, this will amalgamate with the juices and be transformed into a tasty caramelized layer.

Wash the tomatoes and peppers. Cut a small slice off the base and cut off little "lids." Use a melon baller to scoop out the tomatoes and reserve the flesh. Then remove the seeds and membranes from the peppers.

Dry-fry the pine nuts followed by the chopped almonds. In another skillet, fry the chopped onion for 3 minutes in 3½ tbsp oil. Add the rice, stir rapidly, then add the raisins, chopped garlic, chopped scallions, cinnamon, pine nuts, and almonds.

Add the reserved tomato flesh and stir. Pour in just enough water and diluted tomato juice to cover the mixture. Leave to cook for 10–12 minutes, stirring regularly to prevent it from sticking.

Peppers from Samos

Chop the mint and add to the rice when it is tender and the juices have been absorbed. Season to taste, and give the mixture a final stir.

Arrange the tomatoes and peppers in an ovenproof dish. Smear the insides with a little sugar, then fill them with the rice stuffing.

Put the "lids" back on the stuffed peppers and tomatoes. Pour a generous dash of olive oil over each one. Place in an oven preheated to 375° F/190° C for 50–60 minutes, basting regularly with the oil and the cooking juices. Serve hot or cold scattered with chopped parsley.

Fish & Seafood

Sea Perch with

Preparation time:	*40 minutes*
Cooking time:	*1 hour*
Difficulty:	✸✸

Serves 4

4 portions	sea perch (sea bass)
	salt
	pepper
3	onions
3 cloves	garlic
4	potatoes

8	ripe tomatoes
2	zucchini
2	eggplants
1	leek
	olive oil
1 bunch	dill
1 bunch	parsley

Konstantinos and Chrysanthi Stamkopoulos have been running a restaurant for many years that they have named after Apollo, the Greek god of the sun. They share with you now one of their own recipes, oven-baked sea perch surrounded by tasty, juicy, colorful vegetables. This generous dish is popular with families, and is just right for sharing.

In Greece, sea perch (known as sea bass in the Atlantic) is almost always served broiled, accompanied by vegetables that are cooked separately. This noble fish is particularly prized along European coasts. It has a long head, a big mouth, and a tapered body. The back is grayish-black, the sides are silver, and the belly is white. Measuring 16–40 inches/40–100 centimeters, the average weight is 3½ pounds/1.5 kilograms, although it can weigh as much as 26 pounds/12 kilograms! Found in shallow waters, this solitary fish swims around the coastline and estuaries in the summer. You could also use sea bream, mackerel, or any other fish, providing the flesh will hold its shape in the liquid from cooking the vegetables.

Eggplants, potatoes, tomatoes, zucchini, onions, garlic, and leeks are all used in this dish. The Greeks eat more vegetables than anybody else in Europe. Their hot sunny climate and the many meat-free days stipulated by the Orthodox religious calendar have encouraged cooks to be inventive. They like to serve their vegetables with a range of different sauces. The addition of pickles, a generous dash of olive oil, and long simmering times are usually all it takes to show off these colorful, tasty vegetables.

To make sure the dish looks appetizing and that each ingredient is uniformly browned, we have fried them separately in just a very small quantity of oil. They could, however, all go into one big skillet or ovenproof dish so that they all brown at the same time.

Scrape the scales off the sea perch using a small knife. Using scissors, slit the belly of the fish lengthwise, gut and clean it. Turn the hard interiors of the gills inside out and cut them off. Wash the fish thoroughly.

Season the sea perch with salt and pepper both inside and outside.

Peel the onions, garlic and potatoes and cut them into slices. Set the onions to one side. Next wash and slice the tomatoes, zucchini, and the unpeeled eggplants, together with the leek. Fry each vegetable separately in a small amount of oil.

Vegetables – Apollo Style

Fry the onion rings in oil and when they start to turn brown add chopped dill and parsley. Set to one side.

Put slices of fried eggplant and tomato on the bottom of an ovenproof dish. Lay the fish on top, then arrange the slices of fried potato, zucchini, and leeks around the fish.

Scatter the onions and herbs on top of the fish, finishing with more slices of tomato. Sprinkle with any chopped parsley or dill that is left over. Put into an oven preheated to 350° F/180° C for 30–40 minutes.

Angler Fish and Mussels

Preparation time: 30 minutes
Cooking time: 10 minutes
Difficulty: ★

Serves 4

1 lb 2 oz/500 g	angler fish (monkfish)
4 tbsp	olive oil
1	onion
1	small green chile
2 cloves	garlic
	salt
	pepper
2 tsp	flour

10 oz/300 g	mussels
3 tbsp	white wine
⅓ cup/20 g	breadcrumbs
½ bunch	parsley
½ bunch	dill (optional)
4 oz/115 g	zucchini
1 tbsp	sweet mustard
1	lemon

For the garnish (optional):

thin slivers of red
bell pepper

Thessalonika, also known as Salonika, is a magnificent city with a prestigious past, its Mediterranean-style façades looking out to sea. In this city founded by Cassandra, King of Macedonia, 325 years before Christianity arrived in Greece, fish dishes have always been particularly popular with the locals. Angler fish (monkfish) and mussels fried with zucchini is a traditional, succulent dish in this part of Greece, usually eaten as a hot appetizer.

Every day boats from the little fishing villages dotted around Thessalonika bring in their catches of top quality fish to be sold in the local markets. The angler fish is very highly prized in Greece. It lives on the sandy and clayey seabed around the coast. Its dense, delicate, and juicy flesh, which tastes like lobster, can be cooked in lots of different ways. Depending on the time of year, our chef says you could also use whiting or even cod.

This particular specialty also stars mussels. Known as *mydia* by the locals, most are collected in the Pieria area of Macedonia. Famed for their tasty flesh, these mollusks are often served as part of a *mezze*, accompanied by an aperitif. Cleaned and shelled by hand, great quantities of Pieria mussels can be found in the markets in Athens and Thessalonika. If you are using fresh ones, be particularly careful when you sort through them, making sure you discard any that have broken shells or that are half open. Before cooking mussels, remove the beards and any filaments then scrub them under plenty of running water, discarding any that are open or don't shut after a sharp tap with a knife.

This bright and cheerful looking dish pays homage to the flavors of summer. Zucchini, so loved by Mediterranean people, are complemented with the distinctive flavors of parsley and dill, which all blend wonderfully with the angler fish and the mussels.

Skin the angler fish. Using a knife, re-move the central bone then slice the flesh into medallions of equal thickness.

Heat 2 tbsp olive oil in a skillet and fry the finely chopped onion, finely sliced chile, and 1 crushed clove of garlic. Season the medallions of fish with salt and pepper, sprinkle with 1 tbsp flour and fry in 2 tbsp olive oil until golden. Set aside.

Clean the beards off the mussels and tip them into the onion, chile, and garlic mix-ture. Add the medallions of angler fish.

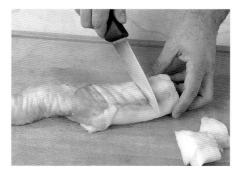

Fried with Zucchini

Pour over the white wine, cover, and cook for 3 minutes. Remove the mussels, discarding any unopened ones. Cook for 2 minutes, then remove the fish and strain the stock. Shell the mussels.

Mix the breadcrumbs, remaining crushed garlic, and 2 sprigs each of chopped parsley and dill. Spread over the fish. Cut the zucchini into very thin slices and blanch in boiling salted water for about 1 minute.

Add a little water and 1 tsp flour to the reserved stock and blend with a whisk. Add the mustard and lemon juice. Stir well then sprinkle with the remaining chopped parsley and dill. Arrange the angler fish, mussels, and zucchini on a plate. Pour over the sauce, and garnish.

Squid

Preparation time:	40 minutes		10	tomatoes
Cooking time:	35 minutes		1 pinch	sugar
Difficulty:	☆		2	bay leaves
			16	medium squid (calamari)

Serves 4

4	onions
4 cloves	garlic
	olive oil for frying
4–5 stems	flat-leaf parsley
4–5 sprigs	cilantro (coriander)
4–5 sprigs	dill
	salt
	pepper

To serve (optional):

1 cup/200 g	Basmati rice
1 cup/250 ml	chicken stock
2 oz/55 g	butter
	salt
	pepper

In this dish, which is very popular with Greeks, the squid *plaki* are cooked in the oven in a tomato sauce. The Greek Orthodox Church prohibits the eating of meat on Mondays, Wednesdays, and Fridays, as well as at certain times of the year such as before Easter and Christmas. People traditionally eat vegetables, herbs, and rice on these days, as well as seafood, providing they have no blood. Cuttlefish, squid, and octopus are thus perfectly acceptable to eat on such days. Since Greece has over 9,000 miles/15,000 kilometers of coastline and thousands of islands, these are all readily available at the market. They are often served fried, stuffed, or simmered in tomato sauce or red wine.

To make squid *plaki*, you could use baby squid that you will be able to cook and serve whole. You don't need to gut them. Just remove the eyes, the horned beak, and the central translucid bone. If they are bigger ones, though, it is best to poach them whole, then cut them up and skin them afterward. This method makes it much easier to handle the squid.

In our recipe the tentacles are cut off but are used later in the recipe. To remove the beak of the squid, poke a finger under the central part of the crown of the tentacles, squeeze the hard part upward, and cut it off with scissors.

If the tomatoes used to make the sauce are a bit bland or lacking in color, you can improve both by adding some tomato paste and a pinch of sugar. Greeks like to use the small tomatoes grown in the Cyclades with their bright red, smooth skins, which are packed with flavor. You can also add some white wine to your sauce.

A pilau rice cooked in butter and stock goes well with squid *plaki*. Garnish the rice and squid with the tentacles, bay leaf, and dill.

Peel and roughly chop the onions and garlic. Brown them for 5 minutes in oil in a pan. When they start to soften add chopped parsley, cilantro and dill, and season with salt and pepper. Stir and continuing cooking.

Peel and roughly chop the tomatoes and add to the fried onions with a pinch of sugar, salt and pepper to taste, and a bay leaf. Leave to cook for 10–15 minutes.

Meanwhile bring water to the boil in a big pan, plunge in the squids, and cook covered for 5 minutes.

Plaki

Cut the tentacles off the cooked squid and discard the beak. Gut the squid, removing the translucid central bone (cartilage), and skin. Wash the tentacles and mantles thoroughly.

Slice the squid mantles into even-sized rings.

Arrange the squid rings and tentacles in an ovenproof dish. Cover with the onion and tomato sauce. Put the dish under the broiler for 10 minutes. Serve with pilau rice (see above for ingredients).

Squid Stuffed with Mastelo

Preparation time:	*15 minutes*
Cooking time:	*5 minutes*
	+ barbe-
	cuing time
Difficulty:	☆

Serves 4

4	red Florina peppers
4 slices	*mastelo* cheese (or mozzarella)
4	large squid
	salt
1 tbsp	olive oil

For the sauce:

1 clove	garlic
3–4 tbsp	olive oil
1 tbsp	all-purpose flour
2	lemons
	salt
½ bunch	parsley

For the garnish:

	lemon zest

In the traditional religious calendar of the Greek Orthodox Church, there are many days on which the faithful are prohibited from eating meat, and in order to honor this ruling, Greek families often eat squid instead. The recipe for this hot appetizer comes from the island of Chios.

Squid are found in huge numbers around the Aegean coast. Usually measuring about 20 inches/50 centimeters long, they are recognizable by their spindle-shaped bodies covered with blackish membranes. They are usually eaten broiled, fried, or stuffed. Cousins of the cuttlefish, which you could alternatively use, they are valued for their flesh.

This carefully planned seafood recipe awards an equally important role to red Florina peppers. Grown exclusively in the Florina area of western Macedonia, they are very sweet and the Greeks love them. In earlier times they were used primarily in the manufacture of powdered red peppers which used to be exported throughout Europe and the Balkans. These days they are steeped in vinegar and sold in jars. If you can't find Florina peppers you can use fresh red bell peppers instead. Before stuffing them, broil them for about 10 minutes so you can peel the skins. You also need to carefully remove the seeds and membrane, making sure the peppers retain their original shape.

In this summer dish, *mastelo* cheese adds the finishing touch. This cheese is produced in the plains around Chios and is still made by hand. Our chef suggests you use mozzarella if you can't find *mastelo*.

Serve with a sauce made from parsley and olive oil. Stefanos Kovas wanted to introduce an additional touch of color, so he has added some strips of lemon zest pared from the rind. Don't forget to blanch the strips in two lots of boiling water.

Prepare the Florina peppers as outlined above. Cut the cheese into 4 triangles, stuffing one inside each pepper.

Cut off the head and tentacles from the squid and gently empty out the innards and cartilage from the mantle. Set aside the tentacles. Peel off the skin and wash the mantles and wings.

Insert the stuffed peppers into the squid mantles. Add the chopped tentacles.

Cheese and Florina Peppers

Pick up the squid in your hand and insert toothpicks at intervals to close over the opening. Salt it, brush lightly with olive oil, and grill over a barbecue. For the garnish, pare off the lemon peel with a zester or sharp knife and blanch it twice.

To make the sauce, brown the whole, peeled garlic clove in the olive oil. Remove the garlic clove, add the flour, and blend with a whisk. Add ⅔ cup/150 ml water, whisking constantly, and add the juice of the lemons and a little salt.

Sprinkle chopped parsley into the sauce. Cut the squid into thick rounds. Serve with the sauce poured round the squid, garnished with the lemon zest.

Squid Stuffed with

Preparation time:	*40 minutes*
Cooking time:	*45 minutes*
Marinating time (squid):	*30 minutes*
Difficulty:	★★

Serves 6

6	squid, each about 10 oz/300 g
1	lemon
3 oz/85 g	onions
3 oz/85 g	tomatoes
3 oz/85 g	red bell peppers

3 oz/85 g	green bell peppers
4 oz/115 g	*kefalotyri* cheese
	salt
	pepper
¾ cup/175 ml	extra-virgin olive oil

By filling the squid with peppers and cheese, Miltos Karoubas is sharing one of the Greek's most favorite ways of enjoying these mollusks. A delight for the eye and the taste buds, the stuffing enhances the slightly bland taste of the squid and helps to soften them.

Squid are part of a culinary heritage that dates back to Ancient Greece. When cooking them, Greek cooks usually pull off the head and the organs come away at the same time. Our chef, however, uses a knife to make a cut high up on the mantle then cleans out the squid and removes the translucid central bone at the same time. After skinning them, and washing them carefully to remove any sand or impurities, rub a slice of lemon into the mantles and the tentacles. Leave to marinate for 30 minutes so that the flesh absorbs the flavor of the lemon, the acidity of which also turns the flesh white.

The squids in this recipe are garnished with a savory mix of bell peppers, tomatoes, onions, and cheese. Bell peppers are closely associated with Mediterranean cookery these days, and were first imported from the Americas in the 16th century. They are available in a wide range of colors and varieties, from green to bright red, orange or pale yellow. Choose peppers that are firm to the touch and that have unwrinkled, bright shiny skins. You can keep them for eight days in the refrigerator.

The *kefalotyri* used to stuff the squid is one of the most popular cheeses in Greece. Hard and salty, it works well in stuffings and with pasta, and is a great addition to pie fillings.

The stuffed squid are usually served whole, each guest eating them as they like. A more elegant way of serving them is to slice them into medallions so that all of the ingredients used to stuff them are on view.

Cut the tentacles off the squid. Make a cut around the mantles then remove the head, internal organs, central bone, and the gray skin. Rinse the mantles and tentacles under running water.

Rub the squid mantles and tentacles with slices from half the lemon and leave to marinate for 30 minutes.

Peel and finely chop the onions. Cut the tomatoes into small half-moon sections. Cut open the bell peppers, remove the seeds and membranes, and cut the flesh into thin strips.

Vegetables and Kefalotyri

Lay out the squid mantles on a cutting board. Stuff them with the strips of bell pepper, finely chopped onions, then the sections of tomato and sticks of kefalotyri cheese.

When the squid are filled, close the ends using 3 or 4 toothpicks. Season them and place under a broiler for 45 minutes on moderate heat, turning them from time to time.

In a bowl whisk the olive oil with the salt and pepper and the juice of half a lemon until it turns into a sauce. Put one stuffed squid on each plate and pour over the sauce.

Sea Bream with Celery

Preparation time:	*20 minutes*
Cooking time:	*35 minutes*
Salting time (sea bream):	*15 minutes*
Difficulty:	★

Serves 4

4	gray sea bream, each about 1 lb 9 oz/ 700 g, cleaned and gutted
	salt
1 scant cup/ 100 g	all-purpose flour

scant ½ cup/ 100 ml	virgin olive oil
1	medium red onion
1 head	celery
1	small celeriac root
	freshly ground black pepper
3	eggs
3	lemons

Located to the south of Epirus, the port of Preveza opens onto the Gulf of Amvrakiko, a particularly famous fishing area. An enormous choice of fish and shellfish is available at Preveza market, some from the Gulf of Amvrakiko and some from the Ionian Sea. Our chef is pleased to bring you this recipe for gray sea bream flavored with celery and coated in *avgolemono*, a popular sauce made from eggs and lemons that Greeks add to a whole range of dishes.

Since royal sea bream is unknown in Greece, cooks use the gray variety instead. This coastal fish, a member of the sparid family, measures 8–16 inches/20–40 centimeters in length and weighs 10 ounces–4½ pounds/(300 grams–2 kilograms). Its white lean flesh is highly prized by gourmets. Smaller sea bream weighing 10–12 ounces/300–350 grams are known as *kotses* in Greek. The big ones, which is what we are using in our recipe, are known as *tsipoures*.

Only the leaves from the celery stalk will be used to add flavor and color to the recipe. You can choose either a white or red variety of onion, although our chef prefers the red ones which he thinks taste better.

When the sea bream is being cooked with the celery and onion, use some of the cooking juices to baste the fish at regular intervals so that it doesn't dry out. This will also impregnate the flesh with the flavor of the vegetables.

The *avgolemono* sauce poured over the fish at the last minute takes its name from the words *avgo* ("eggs") and *lemoni* ("lemon"). Particularly popular in the Ionian region, it is used to coat fish or meat, and is also added to soups. Our chef recommends that you don't pour it cold over the fish, because it will curdle. Warm it up a little instead by blending in some of the warm cooking liquid so that it is the same temperature as the fish.

Wash the sea bream. Place in a colander, salt them and leave to rest for 15 minutes. Then coat in flour.

Heat 3–4 tbsp oil in a heavy-bottomed pan. Put the fish into the hot oil and fry on one side for 5 minutes, then turn with a palette knife to brown on the other side.

In a large, shallow pan, fry the chopped red onion in olive oil. Add the celery leaves, the peeled and cubed celeriac, a cup of water, salt and pepper. Cover and cook for 15 minutes (moving the mixture around while it is cooking to prevent it from sticking to the bottom of the pan).

and Avgolemono Sauce

Lay the fried sea bream on top of the vegetables and bring to the boil (add a little water if necessary). You may have to do this in batches, depending on the size of the fish and your pan.

Meanwhile whisk the eggs in a bowl until they are foaming, add the juice of 3 lemons and a little of the warm cooking juices and whisk rapidly.

Pour the sauce over the fish, check the seasoning and serve hot.

Fillet of

Preparation time: 40 minutes
Cooking time: 30 minutes
Marinating time (fish): 10 minutes
Difficulty: ✶

Serves 4

2	wild artichokes (or poivrade artichokes)
1	lemon
2	onions
1	leek
½ bunch	celery
3–4 tbsp	olive oil

	salt
	pepper
4	angler fish (monkfish) fillets

For the marinade:

	salt
	white pepper
1 clove	garlic
1	lemon
3–4 tbsp	white wine
2 tbsp	olive oil

For the garnish:

	few sprigs dill

Extremely light, fillet of angler fish *aguinarato* is a very popular dish in the Greek islands. A judicious blend of fish and wild vegetables, this specialty from the coast is given a lift by the sharp tang of the lemon.

Easy to make, it can be enjoyed on any occasion. Found on the sandy or clayey seabeds of the Mediterranean, the angler fish is also known as monkfish or goose fish in the Atlantic. Prized for its firm, delicate, and juicy flesh, this fish can be cooked in a wide range of ways. In this recipe it needs to be marinated for about ten minutes in white wine, lemon, garlic, olive oil, salt, and white pepper. You could also use grouper, another popular fish.

This recipe is extremely subtle and full of spring flavors. In Greek cookery, the term *aguinarato* means a preparation based on artichokes and other wild vegetables, but always cooked with lemon. Specific to this region, artichokes have been used in hundreds of recipes from time immemorial.

Greeks usually go out as a family to pick the delicately flavored little artichokes that grow in the fields. They grow wild in some Mediterranean countries, but like our chef you could also use the poivrade variety. These small pale mauve artichokes can be recognized from their pretty violet-green color that sometimes almost looks tinted. Extremely tender, they can also be eaten raw. Choose ones that still have their leaves intact, with no blemishes and are good and firm.

Inseparable from the term *aguinarato*, the lemon enlivens the flavors of the other ingredients. Extremely refreshing, it is also recognized for its vitamin C content. In Greece, virtually every garden has a lemon tree!

Remove the leaves of the artichokes until you reach the core, and remove the choke. Put the halved cores into a bowl of water with some slices of lemon. Wash the vegetables and cut the onions and the leek into very small pieces. Slice the celery. Reserve the lemon slices.

Heat the olive oil in an ovenproof dish. Add the onions and let them brown. Add the leek, artichokes, and celery. Season and cover with water. Cook for 5–10 minutes.

Use a sharp knife to clean the fish fillets and skin them. Cut them into regular sized slices.

Angler Fish Aguinarato

For the marinade: Lay the fish fillets on a plate. Season, add the chopped garlic, lemon juice, and white wine. Turn the fish so they are well coated then add the olive oil and leave to marinate for 10 minutes.

Remove the fillets from the marinade; reserve the marinade. Place the fillets on top of the vegetables and cook for about 1 minute.

Add the marinade to the fish together with the reserved slices of lemon. Cook in an oven preheated to 300° F/150° C for about 20 minutes. Arrange the angler fish aguinarato on a serving plate and garnish with sprigs of dill.

Preparation time: 45 minutes
Cooking time: 30 minutes
Difficulty: ★★

Serves 4

1	turbot weighing 4½ lb/2 kg
1	bay leaf
1	carrot
1	onion
1 stalk	celery
10 oz/300 g	fennel bulbs
⅔ cup/150 ml	olive oil
5 oz/150 g	pearl onions

1 clove	garlic
	salt
	pepper
1 sprig	thyme
¾ cup/200 ml	white wine
1	egg yolk
2	lemons

For the garnish:

fennel leaves

A particularly popular fish among Cretans and the inhabitants of northeastern Greece, this recipe marries turbot (*kalkani*) and fennel with great flair. An extremely elegant summer dish, it is ideal to share with friends.

Greek cookery provides a wonderful showcase for fish and shellfish caught in local waters. Even when just broiled and served with a dash of olive oil, aromatic herbs, and lemon juice, the taste is outstanding.

Kalkani with fennel is a perfect illustration of this. Enjoyed since the days of Ancient Greece for its white, firm and particularly delicate flesh, turbot is regarded by Greeks as the king of flat fish. Depending on the catch, however, you could replace it with any other sea fish provided it has a more robust taste than farmed fish. You could also replace the turbot with tilapia. Don't forget to keep the head and the trimmings for making the stock.

This subtle and carefully thought out dish allows the aniseed flavor of the fennel to shine through. This umbelliferous plant can grow up to 6 feet/1.8 meters tall and it flourishes in the sandy soil of the Mediterranean coast. Widely available in Greek markets in winter, fennel is renowned for its high vitamin C content.

In ancient times, Hippocrates and Dioscorides recommended it to their patients! Try to find small ones because they will be more tender, white and crisp. Our chef suggests you also try this recipe with young Swiss chard leaves.

The crowning touch to this dish of turbot with fennel is an *avgolemono* sauce. Typically Greek, the sauce is made from beaten egg, olive oil, lemon juice, salt, pepper, and a little of the reserved fish stock, which should be added while still warm. Rich and smooth, it is traditionally added to soups and a wide range of seafood dishes.

Using a sharp knife, gently fillet the turbot. Remove the trimmings and the head and set aside for the fish stock.

Pour 4 cups/1 l water into a pan with the bay leaf and peeled and roughly chopped carrot, onion, and celery. Add the turbot trimmings and head and cook for 20 minutes, then strain the stock and put to one side.

Wash the fennel bulbs and cut into equal slices with a knife.

Fennel

Heat 2 tbsp olive oil in a pan and brown the chopped pearl onions and crushed garlic clove. Add the fennel, seasoning, and scatter the mixture with thyme leaves. Pour on the white wine and top up the liquid with stock so that it just covers the vegetables. Cook for 3 minutes.

Season the turbot fillets. Heat 1 tbsp olive oil in a skillet and brown the fillets on their skin side. Add the fish (with the skin side uppermost) to the fennel mixture. Cook for 2 minutes. Reserve the cooking liquid.

In a bowl, beat the egg yolk then add the remaining olive oil and the lemon juice. Season. Add a little of the reserved cooking liquid. Stir well, pour around the turbot and fennel and serve garnished with fennel leaves.

May-time

Preparation time: 45 minutes
Cooking time: 45 minutes
Difficulty: ★★

Serves 4

	salt
2	carrots
2	onions
1 head	celery
	red wine vinegar
2	bay leaves
2	lobsters, each 2½ lb/1 kg

scant ½ cup/ 100 ml	olive oil
10	scallions
1 lb 5 oz/600 g	button mushrooms
2½ lb/1 kg	tomatoes
	pepper
1 bunch	flat-leaf parsley
1	lemon

In choosing this typical dish from Mytilene, George Anastassakis brings together seafood, the gift of Poseidon, the god of the sea, and vegetables, the gift of Demeter, the goddess of the harvest. Greeks are particularly fond of dishes that use crustaceans and fresh vegetables.

In May, the fishermen from Mytilene bring back their catches of wonderfully succulent lobsters from the Aegean Sea, and cook them with scallions and other spring vegetables from their gardens. Hence the name they have given this recipe – *astakos mayatikos* or "May-time lobsters."

The Greeks have been eating fish and seafood for thousands of years. Even in the days of Pericles (450 B.C.), lobster was already on the menu at Athenian banquets, as were oysters, shrimp, mussels, and sole. In Greece, lobsters are these days often poached in a *court bouillon* and served with mayonnaise, or simply grilled over the barbecue.

There are several ways of cooking a lobster. Our chef puts it onto a long flat metal tray (supplied with the fish kettle) and firmly attaches it by winding string around both lobster and tray. Using the handles, he can then plunge the lobster into the hot *court bouillon* without it moving, then easily lift it out again. You can, however, just put it into boiling water without any kind of support. When it is removed from the stock it will need to be left to cool down before being shelled. (Before they cook it, other cooks prefer to plunge the blade of a sharp, heavy knife in the cross-hatch right behind its head. After doing so, the lobster should be placed in the freezer for a few minutes while muscular contractions "empty it out.")

The mushrooms and onions are simmered in just a single glassful of the cooking liquid, and any that is left over will be reused as a delicious base for a fish soup or sauce.

In a fish kettle, add water, salt, peeled and sliced carrots and onions, stems and leaves of chopped celery, dash of wine vinegar, and 1 bay leaf. Cover, bring to the boil, then drop the lobsters into the liquid and let them cook for 20–25 minutes.

Remove the cooked lobsters from the liquid, put them onto a cutting board and leave them to cool down before you remove the shells.

Cut the 2 tails into medallions.

Lobsters

Put the olive oil, ¾ cup/200 ml strained stock from cooking the lobsters, chopped scallions and mushrooms into a pan, and leave to simmer for about 10 minutes.

Peel and chop the tomatoes. Add to the mushrooms with salt, pepper, and chopped parsley and cook for about another 5 minutes.

Add the medallions of lobster to the vegetables. Reheat for 3 minutes over a brisk heat. Arrange a bed of vegetables on the serving dish with the medallions on top. Decorate with the bay leaf and some lemon.

Broiled Sea Perch with

Preparation time: 35 minutes
Cooking time: 25 minutes
Difficulty: ★★

Serves 4

4	large artichokes
1	lemon
12	small potatoes
12	small carrots
12	pearl onions
3½ oz/ 100 g	peas
1	sea perch (sea bass) weighing 2½ lb/1.2 kg
	salt, pepper

For the sauce:

3 cloves	garlic
3	basil leaves
½ tsp	sweet mustard
	salt
	pepper
1 pinch	saffron
2 tbsp	white wine
1	lemon
2 tbsp	olive oil
3	blood oranges

For the garnish:

	capers
	dill sprigs
	basil leaves

Extremely light to digest, this recipe is an invitation to discover the riches of Greek cuisine. A particular favorite on the islands, sea perch (known as bass in the Atlantic) is traditionally flavored with olive oil and lemon. Easy to make, this summer dish concentrates several Mediterranean flavors in a marvelous way.

Worthy heirs of Ulysses, the Greeks always have their eyes turned to the sea. Sought out by fish lovers for its fine, dense but delicate flesh, the Mediterranean sea perch has great character. Relatively fragile, it needs only a short cooking time. When bought fresh, it should still be rigid, have shiny scales and pink gills. Depending on the catch, you could replace it with sea bream.

This delicate recipe is served with spring vegetables. Our chef likes to enrich the original recipe with artichokes.

Usually cooked with lemon, olive oil, and dill they are eaten either as a hot appetizer or a main course.

Peas, another of the spring vegetables used in this dish, have been enjoyed since the days of Ancient Greece. They are grown in many vegetable gardens and can be found in the market in summer. Look out for ones that have a bright green pod that is intact, hard and plump. They keep for two or three days in the refrigerator, but it is best to use them as quickly as you can. You could also use some fresh fava beans, or English broad beans.

Aristedes Pasparakis is passionate about Greek produce and had the idea of serving the broiled fish with a sauce made from blood oranges flavored with basil. These oranges are grown widely in the Peloponnese, their slightly tart taste adding a real lift to this wonderful fish dish.

Peel the artichokes, removing the leaves until you get to the choke. Holding onto the stem, remove the choke with a melon baller. Dip the artichoke hearts into a bowl of water to which slices of lemon have been added.

Peel the potatoes, carrots, and pearl onions. Shell the peas. Cut the carrots into batons.

Heat a pan of salted water then add the potatoes and carrots. Cook for 5 minutes before adding the pearl onions and sliced artichoke hearts. Cook for a further 5 minutes, add the peas, and cook for another 5 minutes. Drain and refresh the vegetables in iced water.

Blood Orange Sauce

Clean out and fillet the sea perch. Season the fillets, then dry-fry them in a nonstick skillet.

To make the sauce, put finely sliced cloves of garlic, chopped basil leaves, and the mustard into a salad bowl and season. Add the saffron to the white wine, lemon juice, and olive oil. Stir well and add to the mustard sauce.

Squeeze the oranges. Heat the sauce mixture, add the juice from the blood oranges and allow the sauce to reduce a little. Pass the sauce through a strainer. Pour the sauce and the vegetables around the fish and garnish with capers, dill, and basil leaves.

Whiting

Preparation time: 30 minutes
Cooking time: 10 minutes
Difficulty: ☆

Serves 4

6	small whiting
2	lemons
2 tsp	thyme leaves
	salt
	pepper

1 bunch	flat-leaf parsley
2 cloves	garlic
12	grape (vine) leaves
	olive oil

For the garnish:

thyme sprigs
lemon

For his restaurant in Vouliagmeni, Anastasios Tolis is able to buy the most succulent fish unloaded in Pireus, the biggest port in Greece. He brings you this very simple recipe for broiled whiting wrapped in grape leaves, known as vine leaves across Europe.

Whiting is one of the most widely used fish in Greece. They have a torpedo shaped body about 10–20 inches/25–50 centimeters long, and they belong to the same family as haddock and cod. They have a prominent upper jaw, a greenish-gray back and a black mark at the base of their pectoral fins. Their fine flesh can be easily filleted into thin slices. To ensure they are fresh, choose ones with bright eyes, with skin that is more yellow than gray, and with a belly that is still very white. For our recipe they can be replaced with small cod or very big sardines. Wrapping the fish in grape leaves gives the whiting a welcome freshness, particularly when they are barbecued in the summer.

In 1000 B.C., cooks were using fig leaves to wrap around various foodstuffs, but these had been replaced with grape leaves by the Byzantine Age.

These days, grape leaves are generally preserved (and sold) in brine so they need careful washing before they are used. However, if you have the chance to find fresh, untreated leaves, remove the tough part of the stem and steam them. Greeks love to use them to wrap around stuffing mixes made from rice and herbs, as well as fish, whether whole or filleted.

Our chef has cooked his whiting over a grill (gas, barbecue, etc.) but you could also bake them in the oven, allowing about 5–6 minutes on each side. To flavor them, just arrange slices of lemon and a generous sprig of thyme on top. Serve with a medley of colorful vegetables.

Slice open the bellies of the whiting. Clean them out, remove the central bone and the insides of the gills. Wash them thoroughly.

Season the fish with lemon juice, thyme leaves, salt and pepper.

Open up each fish and fill it with a mixture of chopped flat-leaf parsley, chopped garlic, salt and pepper.

Abelofila

Line up and slightly overlap 2 washed/prepared grape leaves on a chopping board. Lay one fish on top and fold the leaves around it. Wrap the other 5 fish in the same way.

Lay the wrapped fish on top of a grill rack and put a plate or a board underneath. Brush the fish all over with olive oil.

Cook them over a hot barbecue for 5 minutes on each side. Serve while still hot, garnished with fresh thyme and slices of lemon.

Fish Stuffed with

Preparation time: 50 minutes
Cooking time: 20 minutes
Difficulty: ★★

Serves 4

1	sea bream weighing 3½–4½ lb/1.5–2 kg
1	carrot
1	zucchini
1	green bell pepper
1	red bell pepper
1	orange bell pepper
2	oyster mushrooms
3–4 tbsp	white wine
3 tbsp	olive oil
2	tomatoes
	salt

In Greek cookery, fish dishes are legion and around the islands top-quality fish can be cooked in many different ways. In summer, families living on the coast get together to enjoy this specialty bursting with wonderful flavors.

The concept of fish stuffed with sun-ripened vegetables goes back thousands of years. The Greeks usually use a special tile called a *keramida* on which to cook this dish, and every household has one. The fish is then served direct to the guests at the table.

Found primarily in the waters of the Mediterranean and the Atlantic, sea bream is a special favorite for its white, lean, and fine flesh. Somewhat fragile, it only needs a short cooking time. You could replace it with sea perch (sea bass).

Full of vitamins, another starring role in this dish goes to the bell peppers. The epitome of sun-ripened vegetables, market stalls come alive with color when bell peppers are in season. Whether red, green, yellow, or orange, they are all the fruit of the capsicum.

Green bell peppers, which are harvested before they are fully ripe, have a thick, crunchy flesh. Their flavor is slightly sweet and piquant. The red ones are more fragile, but they have a smooth taste with no bitterness. They are particularly good for salads, stews, pasta, and rice dishes. The orange and yellow ones have thick flesh and these too are very sweet. Choose ones that are hard, smooth, have no blemishes, and a green and stiff stalk.

As for the zucchini, they contain a lot of water and are very low in calories. Zucchini can be eaten with or without their skins, although you are recommended to scrape the skins if you're not planning to peel them. Look for the small ones because the bigger ones are often full of seeds.

Prepare the sea bream by scraping off the scales. Using a knife, make an incision in the back so you can clean it out and remove the central bone.

Peel the carrot, wash the zucchini and the bell peppers, removing the seeds and white membrane from the latter. Cut all the vegetables into julienne strips.

Cut the oyster mushrooms into pieces. Put them in a large pan with the white wine and bring to the boil.

Sun-ripened Vegetables

Heat 3 tbsp olive oil in a skillet. Add the julienne strips of vegetable, cook for 5 minutes, add diced tomatoes, and the mushrooms. Season with salt.

Salt the inside of the sea bream and stuff with the vegetables.

Tie some kitchen string around the sea bream so that it retains its shape and stays quite firm. Place in an ovenproof dish with any remaining vegetables. Cook in an oven preheated to 475° F/240° C for about 15 minutes.

Octopus with

Preparation time:	*20 minutes*
Cooking time (octopus):	*55 minutes*
Cooking time (pasta):	*10 minutes*
Difficulty:	✶

Serves 6

1	octopus weighing 2½ lb/1 kg
	salt
scant ½ cup/ 100 ml	white wine
⅔ cup/150 ml	extra-virgin olive oil
2	onions
3 cloves	garlic
1½ lb/650 g	chopped tomatoes
1 stick	cinnamon
15	black peppercorns
	freshly ground black pepper
½ bunch	parsley
4½ cups/500 g	small macaroni

Located on the very edge of the easternmost island of Chalkidiki in Macedonia, Mount Athos is home to about 20 monasteries and nearly 1,700 Orthodox monks. This octopus stew with small pasta shapes is a recipe that has been adapted for those days on which no meat may be consumed. Having no blood, mollusks can be eaten on these days and this dish has become one of the monks' culinary specialties. It is also enjoyed on the nearby islands.

Octopus, known as *oktapodi* in Greek, means it has eight feet. In fact it has eight tentacles with suckers, all of them the same length, which join at the head. It is particularly abundant in the Aegean Sea. In summer the fishing boats always return with quantities of octopus, squid, and cuttlefish, which are then cooked in lots of different recipes. As the flesh of the octopus is very tough, the fishermen traditionally beat it 44 times against a wall or a rock to tenderize it. The bigger ones are cut into small dice then used in salads or stews, while the little ones are particularly popular broiled. One very old custom involves hanging them on wires to dry so they can be kept for "no meat" days.

Octopus are quite a lot simpler to cook than squid or cuttlefish because they don't need to be gutted. However, make sure you wash any sand out of the sac if this has not already been done by the fishmonger.

Simmered in a pleasantly spicy tomato sauce, our octopus is served with small pasta shapes. Dozens of different sorts of pasta can be bought at Greek markets, all of them called some variety of *macaronia*. The type used by our chef is *macaronia kofta*, "cut macaroni," which looks like small rings. Add these cooked pasta shapes to the stew just before it is served.

Wash the octopus. Put it into a large pan filled with salted water and add the white wine. Bring to the boil and leave to cook for 30 minutes. Drain immediately.

Put the octopus onto a chopping board and cut it into small cubes.

In a pan, briskly fry the pieces of octopus in olive oil, together with chopped onions and garlic. Add the chopped tomatoes.

Small Pasta Shapes

Next add the stick of cinnamon, peppercorns, salt and ground pepper. Add a little oil if necessary and cook for 15–20 minutes. When the octopus is tender add chopped parsley and stir.

During this time cook the pasta for 10 minutes in a separate pan filled with boiling salted water. Drain well.

Add the cooked pasta to the octopus stew. Stir for a moment or two over the heat then serve as quickly as possible.

Saffron Rice with Mussels

Preparation time: 30 minutes
Cooking time: around 25 minutes

Difficulty: ★★

Serves 4

2¼ lb/1 kg	mussels
2 or 3	carrots
1	zucchini
1	onion
2 cloves	garlic
½ cup/125 ml	olive oil

scant ½ cup/100 ml	white wine
scant ½ cup/100 ml	ouzo
3 cups/800 ml	fish stock
1	bay leaf
3 g	saffron
	salt
	pepper
1¾ cups/350 g	long grain rice
1 bunch	arugula (rocket)
2 tbsp	wild dill

In the port of Thessalonika and along the beach at Aretzo, the little restaurants all serve succulent plates of mussels. Comprising of rice, mussels, and vegetables flavored with saffron, the dish our chef is sharing with you is somewhat similar to a Spanish paella.

For thousands of years Greeks have collected mussels off the coast, which they cook with basil, saffron, or just fry. Mussel farms were first developed about 20 years ago in the Pieria region of Macedonia and these days tasty mussels are produced on floating lines.

To cook them, use a knife to scrape off any incrustations that have formed on the shell, then cut off the little black beards. It is vital that you discard any mussels that are still open (they are dead). You can also buy mussels that have already been cleaned and vacuum-packed. Failing this, you could use other shellfish or shrimp for our recipe.

These mussels are cooked with a lot of different flavors, such as ouzo and saffron. This spice was already known in Santorini and Cretan cookery as long ago as 2000 B.C. The poet Homer recounted how the god Jupiter would lie on a bed of saffron, hyacinths, and lotus blossom. Today, 15 percent of the world's production comes from Kozani in western Macedonia. However, always use the threads if you can because the powder is often cut with cartham, curcuma or marigolds.

The ouzo lends its strong aniseed flavor to this recipe. This Greek spirit flavored with aniseed and fennel is consumed at any time of day.

Long grain (Carolina) rice suits this dish well. The Greeks, who themselves grow a little rice in the Larissa district of Thessalia, also import it from different parts of the world. You can choose your favorite from the many varieties.

Scrape the mussel shells to get rid of any incrustations and remove the beards. Cut the ends off the carrots, peel and slice into small batons. Wash the zucchini and cut into batons.

Peel and finely chop the onion and garlic. Heat the olive oil in a large skillet and gently fry the onion, garlic, and carrots.

Arrange the mussels on top of the bed of vegetables in the frying pan and leave them to simmer for 5 minutes.

and Baby Vegetables

Next add the zucchini batons.

Keeping the pan over the heat, stir in the wine, ouzo, fish stock, bay leaf, saffron, and season with salt and pepper. Leave to cook for 4–5 minutes – the liquid should be only just bubbling.

Finally, turn up the heat and add the washed rice. Stir, then leave to cook for about 10 minutes at a rolling boil. Serve hot, garnished with arugula leaves and sprigs of dill.

Tilapia Cooked in

Preparation time: 35 minutes
Cooking time: 25 minutes
Difficulty: ★

Serves 4

1	tilapia weighing 1¾ lb/800 g
1 stalk	celery
1	onion
1	carrot
¾ cup/180 ml	white *malagousia* wine
3–4 tbsp	olive oil
	salt
	pepper

2¼ lb/1 kg	frisée lettuce
2	egg yolks
½	lemon

For the garnish:

fennel leaves

In the culinary traditions of the Aegean islands, fish is always cooked with wild herbs known as *chorta*. Ever since the olden days, the inhabitants have traditionally gathered arugula (rocket), dandelion, chicory in the wild and incorporated them into their cooking with real flair. Tilapia cooked in *malagousia* wine is a typical dish from this part of Greece. Nikos Sarandos decided to adapt it by replacing the wild herbs with a frisée lettuce.

Esteemed for the quality of its white flesh, tilapia is one of the best coastal fish available. (It is also "aquacultured" around the world.) Between 12 and 20 inches/30–50 centimeters long, it is particularly abundant in fall and winter. Firm and smooth, it can be cooked in many ways, but be extra careful when you fillet it because it has some nasty spines. At the fishmonger's choose one that still has its fins in perfect condition, a fat belly, and domed, bright eyes. You could use angler fish (monkfish) or turbot instead.

The fish is marvelously flavored with the aromas of *malagousia* wine. Made from a very fine, white grape, this wine, which is produced in northern Greece, can be replaced with a Chardonnay.

In this recipe, the *malagousia* wine forms a perfect foil for the aniseed taste of the fennel. This umbelliferous plant is called *marathos* in Greek, after the Greek name for the ancient city of Marathon, where it grew in abundance all those thousands of years ago. The Ancient Greeks used it to cure a cough, to improve their eyesight, and to relieve their rheumatism. Rich in vitamin C, fennel has the reputation of being very easy to digest. In this recipe, our chef suggests you could also use dill instead, an aromatic herb that is highly prized in his country.

Fillet the tilapia by cutting off the head and making a long incision along the dorsal bone. Cut the fish into fillets of equal thickness. Carefully clean the head and the bones and reserve.

Make a stock by adding the celery, onion and carrot (all roughly chopped) to a large pan of water. Add the head and the bones of the tilapia. Add 4 tbsp white wine, cook for 20 minutes and skim off any froth that forms.

Strain the stock and transfer it to a pan. Add the olive oil, the rest of the white wine, and season with salt and pepper.

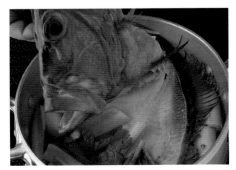

Malagousia Wine

Season the slices of tilapia, then poach them in the stock for about 3 minutes. Reserve the fish and strain the stock again.

Wash the leaves of the frisée lettuce and blanch them for 1 minute in a pan of boiling salted water. Drain the lettuce well and set to one side.

Put the egg yolks in a bowl and whisk in the juice of half a lemon. Add 2 tbsp warm stock while continuing to whisk. Bring the remaining stock to the boil and add the sauce mix. Serve the fish on a bed of lettuce, drizzle over the sauce and garnish with chopped fennel leaves.

Meat & Poultry

Anoghia

Preparation time: 20 minutes
Cooking time: 20 minutes
Difficulty: ★

Serves 4

1	loin of lamb
	salt
	pepper
1	meat bouillon cube
1 lb 2 oz/500 g	spaghetti
4 tbsp	butter

3	sage leaves
3 tbsp	lamb suet
1 tbsp	cornstarch
1 sprig	thyme
1	lemon
5½ oz/150 g	grated *anthotyros* (salted goat milk cheese)

For the garnish:

sage leaves

Anoghia lamb is named after a mountainous region of Crete, which, according to mythology, was the birthplace of Zeus, the supreme god of the Hellenic Pantheon. In this still wild area, farming has bequeathed several original recipes to the island's cuisine. This easy-to-make dish, served here with spaghetti, can be enjoyed any time.

Cretans love broiled meat, and they often cook lamb on a rotating spit known as an *ofto* in the local dialect. They also still use an open fire pit method that would even have been familiar to the Ancient Greeks. The youngest shepherd has the job of clearing the ground then scooping out a hole in the earth. Having made the fire in the pit, it is encircled with stones so that the meat can be laid on top. In summer, you can use the easier method of a barbecue. This dish can also be made with a leg or a shoulder of lamb, depending on your taste.

In the Cretan tradition the meat is always sprinkled with lemon juice. The tartness of the juice gives a lift to the other ingredients. Rich in vitamin C, it is also an ideal addition to soups, sauces, vegetables, stews, and pastries. Lemons originally came from Kashmir and were introduced first to Assyria and later to Greece. Choose fully ripe and blemish-free ones, keeping them in the refrigerator.

Bursting with specifically Cretan flavors, Anoghia Lamb uses an interesting choice of herbs. Thyme grows wild in Mediterranean countries, and whether fresh or dried, it retains its flavor even after it has been cooked.

Sage is also used in this recipe, lending its slightly bitter and piquant power. In the 1st century A.D. Dioscorides, the father of pharmacology, referred to it as *elelisfakon* and praised its medicinal virtues. It is found widely across the whole of Crete.

Using a sharp knife, make a series of cuts in the loin of lamb then use a cleaver to cut it into chops.

Season the chops and put them on a broiler rack over a roasting pan in an oven preheated to 400° F/200° C for about 20 minutes. Reserve the cooking juices in the pan.

Fill a large pan with water and crumble in a meat bouillon cube. Bring to the boil and add the spaghetti. Cook as package instructions and drain well.

Lamb

Melt the butter in a skillet with the sage leaves, then remove the sage leaves.

Transfer the spaghetti to the skillet with the butter and stir over heat. Dilute the reserved cooking juices from the meat with a little water. Add lamb suet, cornstarch, and thyme and stir over heat until it thickens. Season.

Squeeze lemon juice over the chops. Put them on the plate with the spaghetti sprinkled with grated cheese. Drizzle some sauce around the sides of the plate and garnish with sage leaves.

Oven-baked

Preparation time: 20 minutes
Cooking time: 1 hour
     15 minutes
Difficulty: ★

Serves 4

2 whole bulbs	garlic
3¼ lb/1.4 kg	leg of lamb (or mutton)
2	onions
3–4 tbsp	olive oil
	salt
	pepper
2	lemons

1 sprig	thyme
1 sprig	rosemary
1	bay leaf
3¼ kbs/1.5 kg	potatoes
2	tomatoes
2 tbsp	butter (optional)

For the garnish:

	bay leaves
	rosemary

The symbol of reunions, oven-baked *arni* is a dish to be shared with family and friends. This traditional recipe, typical of the hinterland, is usually served to the family on Sunday. In olden days the villagers would take the dish to the local bakehouse to be cooked!

A land of shepherds, Greeks have a special fondness for lamb and for *arni* in particular. Sheep have been raised in the mountainous areas of Greece for centuries and are prized for their delicious meat. You could sometimes ring the changes and use kid goat or pork instead, which are also favorites with the Greeks.

Characteristic of rustic cuisine, oven-baked *arni* is simplicity itself to make and is full of the Mediterranean flavors so loved by Greeks: thyme, rosemary, onion, and bay leaf, which all add flair to the other ingredients.

Lending its own piquancy, cloves of garlic, a plant that grows wild in Greece, are inserted into the meat before cooking. Athletes in Ancient Greek used it as a "stimulant" as it was reputed to add strength and vitality! According to the beliefs of that time, it had to be eaten in the morning. Today the Cyclades are famous for the quality of their garlic. Available all year round on market stalls, the cloves should be hard and firm.

This copious dish also stars vegetables. Potatoes, popular all over the world, soak up the fruity flavor of the olive oil. Originally from the New World, potatoes have been grown in Greece since the beginning of the 20th century. The Livanates region specializes in producing them and today supplies the country's markets.

This succulent oven-baked *arni* is quite simply the Mediterranean sun on a plate!

Break up the garlic bulbs and peel the cloves. Make small slits in the lamb with the tip of a knife and insert individual cloves.

Peel and chop the onions and arrange them in a large roasting pan, sprinkled with a dash of olive oil.

Season the lamb on both sides. Put it on top of the onions and squeeze over the juice of 1 lemon. Add the thyme, rosemary, and bay leaf. Add 1½ tbsp olive oil and ¾ cup/200 ml water. Bake in an oven preheated to 350° F/180° C for about 40 minutes.

Arni

Peel the potatoes and cut into big cubes. Place in a bowl with the remaining olive oil and lemon juice. Season and mix.

Add the potatoes, with their olive oil and lemon juice, to the meat and add ¾ cup water. Cook at the same temperature for about another 20 minutes.

Wash the tomatoes and cut into quarters. Add them to the pan with the meat, together with the butter, if using. Transfer the lamb and vegetables onto a serving dish and garnish with bay leaves and rosemary.

Beef Capama

Preparation time: 20 minutes
Cooking time (beef capama): 1 hour
Cooking time (pilau):   25 minutes
Difficulty: ✷✷

Serves 4

2¼ lb/1 kg	chuck beef
3	medium onions
2 cloves	garlic
scant ½ cup/ 100 ml	olive oil
5 or 6	cloves
1 stick	cinnamon
2	bay leaves
1	orange
¾ cup/200 ml	red wine
	salt, pepper
3	ripe tomatoes
1 tbsp	tomato paste

For the pilau:

4 tbsp	butter
1	small onion
1¾ scant cups/ 300 g	long grain rice
4 cups/1 l	beef stock

For the garnish:

	bay leaf
	orange peel
	cinnamon sticks
	cloves

Distinctive for its powerful taste and aroma of oranges and cinnamon, this beef *capama* is a dish from central northern Greece. This popular and comforting winter stew is served with pilau rice or potatoes. The name *capama* appears to be Turkish, and means "braised."

The mountainous, poor soil of Greece has never been ideal for raising cattle. Only goats and sheep can prosper here because they can climb the steep slopes and graze on the sparse grass. These days cattle are raised in the more verdant areas of the country. So over the centuries, beef has always been a rare and expensive meat reserved for special occasions only.

When making this dish, George Anastassakis usually chooses *moschari*, meat from older calves whose flesh is reddish in color, although this can easily be replaced by brisket or neck of beef. This recipe is also very successful when made with lamb. Greek cooks usually wash the meat under the tap, rubbing it with their fingers. This method of cleaning meat is widely used all around the Mediterranean.

Mixed with garlic and fried onions, the pieces of beef must be left to soften covered in their juices but not browned. They are then simmered in the wine and spices, but you might need to add some water during the cooking time.

Our chef recommends you use Naoussa wine from Macedonia for this dish. The fruit of a variety of vine known as *xynomavro* (black acid), this popular deep red grape has a generous flavor.

To make the pilau, fry the uncooked rice in some butter with the onions. Add twice as much stock to the volume of rice, and leave it to simmer until it swells and is cooked to your liking.

Put the beef onto a chopping board and cut it into big cubes.

Peel and finely chop 2 onions and the garlic. Brown them in olive oil in a heavy-bottomed pan. Add the chunks of beef, cover and braise for about 20 minutes.

Next add the flavorings: 1 onion studded with cloves, the cinnamon stick, bay leaves, orange peel, and red wine. Season and continue cooking for at least 20 minutes.

and Pilau Rice

Add the peeled and chopped tomatoes mixed with a little tomato paste. Cook for a further 15 minutes.

Meanwhile make the pilau. Melt the butter in a large pan, add finely chopped onion, and the rice. Stir for a couple of minutes over the heat to coat the rice.

Pour hot beef stock onto the rice and cook for 20 minutes, until it is fluffy and soft. Serve the meat on a pile of rice garnished with a bay leaf, orange peel, cinnamon and cloves.

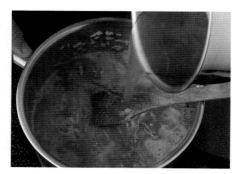

Greek Meatballs

Preparation time: 40 minutes
Cooking time: 30 minutes
Difficulty: ★★

Serves 4–6

For the meatballs:

3	onions
4 cloves	garlic
1 bunch	parsley
7–8 slices/200 g	stale white bread
2¼ lb/1 kg	ground beef
1 tsp	cumin
	salt
	pepper

4	eggs
	flour
	oil for frying

For the tomato sauce:

10	tomatoes
4 cloves	garlic
4 tbsp	olive oil
1 tbsp	sugar
	salt
	pepper
⅔ cup/150 ml	white wine
1 tbsp	flour

Known as *soutsoukakia*, these beef or pork meatballs coated with a tomato sauce are popular throughout Greece. Rolled into plum-sized portions, they are always the same shape – oblong and slightly flattened at each end.

The classic recipe uses ground meat, onions, herbs, and spices, bound with eggs and bread. Always use stale bread with the crusts removed, because fresh bread would be too mushy once it is mixed with the other ingredients. Week-old bread is ideal. If when you mix the meatballs the ingredients are still too wet to be shaped into balls, add a few dry breadcrumbs and that will solve the problem.

It's not always easy to find tomatoes on market stalls that are as ripe as the ones you pick off the vine. You can improve the color and the flavor of the sauce, however, by adding a tablespoon of tomato paste. Likewise, a pinch of sugar will offset any sharpness from tomatoes that are not quite ripe. Chrysanthi Stamkopoulos is also happy to pass on this tip for improving the flavor of the sauce – just add one or two bay leaves and a stick of cinnamon while the sauce is cooking.

Depending on their size, two or three meatballs will be required for each guest. Rice or pasta make the ideal accompaniment. You can serve the meatballs and sauce separately, or use a mold to make a small dome-shaped mound of rice in the middle of each plate with the *soutsoukakia* arranged around the sides and the hot tomato sauce poured over the top. Your guests will be delighted with these little succulent, flavor-filled meatballs.

Meatballs: Peel and finely chop the onions and garlic and combine. Wash and chop the parsley, reserving a few leaves. Remove the crusts from the bread and break it into chunks. In a bowl, mix the ground beef, onions, garlic, parsley, bread, cumin, salt, pepper, and eggs.

Combine all the ingredients with your hands until they are uniformly blended. Shape into oval balls that are about 2–2½ in/5–6 cm long, flattening them slightly at each end.

Coat the meatballs with flour, tapping off the surplus. Heat the oil in a skillet and brown the meatballs for about 10 minutes, turning them so that they become a uniform color.

with Tomato Sauce

To make the sauce, peel the tomatoes, blend to a purée and transfer to a large skillet. Add finely chopped garlic, olive oil, sugar, salt, pepper, and white wine. Bring to the boil and simmer for around 10 minutes.

In a bowl, mix the flour to a smooth paste with a little water and add to the tomato sauce. Stir for 5 minutes over heat to thicken the sauce.

Arrange the fried meatballs in an oven-proof dish. Pour over the tomato sauce and place in an oven preheated to 350° F/180° C for 5 minutes. Serve hot garnished with parsley leaves.

Loin of Lamb with

Preparation time:	*40 minutes*
Cooking time:	*1 hour*
	15 minutes
Soaking time (beans):	*12 hours*
Difficulty:	★

Serves 4

1 cup/200 g	dried white navy (haricot) beans
1	carrot
1 stalk	celery
1	onion
2	tomatoes
1	bay leaf

	salt, pepper
⅔ cup/150 ml	olive oil
2	loins of lamb

For the herb crust:

2 cups/100 g	breadcrumbs
1 clove	garlic (optional)
½ bunch	parsley
½ bunch	dill
1 sprig	rosemary
1	lemon

For the garnish:

	cilantro leaves (coriander)
	cardamom leaves

Full of unrivaled flavors, this loin of lamb with white Kastoria navy (haricot) beans is a traditional recipe from Thessalia and eastern Macedonia. It has a subtle combination of flavors from the land and is mainly served at weddings.

Raised in the mountainous regions of the country, lamb is an essential part of Greek cuisine. Its highly flavored meat is particularly popular when broiled. Our chef suggests you try kid goat, which is also highly prized in Greece.

Wonderfully appetizing to look at, the cutlets are topped with a herb crust made from breadcrumbs, garlic, parsley, dill and rosemary, flavors that are so characteristic of the Mediterranean.

Known since the days of Homer, parsley was used by the warriors in *The Iliad* to feed their horses. This plant, a native of Southern Europe, is available on Greek market stalls all year round and is used to give a lift to many dishes. Choose parsley that has bright green leaves and firm stems.

Dill, meanwhile, or *anithos* as it is known in Greek, is also highly regarded in Greece and Turkey for its aniseed taste. Famous for its culinary and medicinal properties, this plant has a soft and slightly bitter flavor and is often associated with fish and dairy products.

This recipe from the Greek hinterland is simplicity itself to make and also uses navy beans from Kastoria. Famed for its production of pulses, this lovely city in northern Greece is also famous for its furriers' workshops.

Extremely nourishing, dried beans formed part of the staple diet in the Byzantine Age. They need a long cooking time but have the advantage of absorbing the flavors of the other ingredients.

Put the dried beans into a bowl, cover with water, and soak for 12 hours. Drain.

Put the drained beans into a pan of water and simmer briskly for about 1 hour.

Add the carrot, celery, onion, and tomatoes, all cut into small pieces, along with the bay leaf. Season to taste and cook for 10 minutes. Add 3–4 tbsp olive oil and cook for a further 2 minutes.

White Kastoria Beans

Trim the loins of lamb, season, and brown in a scant ½ cup/100 ml olive oil. Roast in an oven preheated to 400° F/200° C for 10 minutes.

To make the herb crust, put the bread-crumbs, garlic, if using, parsley, dill, and rosemary into a food processor and blend. Moisten with lemon juice if dry.

Cover the lamb with the herb crust mixture. Return to the oven for 1 minute. Divide into chops and serve with the beans, garnished with cilantro and cardamom leaves.

Chicken with

Preparation time:	35 minutes
Cooking time:	1 hour
	45 minutes
Difficulty:	★

Serves 4

1	free-range chicken weighing 4½ lb/2 kg
⅔ cup/150 ml	olive oil
1	onion
⅔ cup/150 ml	white wine
1	bay leaf
1 stick	cinnamon

1½ lb/600 g	tomatoes
	salt
	pepper
14 oz/400 g	chilopites (Greek pasta)
½ cup/55 g	grated *myzithra* (goat milk cheese)

Chicken with *chilopites* is a traditional dish in the Greek culinary repertoire. This filling winter dish is very popular throughout the country and is easy to make.

Simmered for a long time with the white wine and other ingredients, the chicken is particularly tasty. Our chef also suggests you try this recipe with beef.

Cleverly put together, this specialty is a wonderful melting pot for the different flavors. Olive oil, such a vital part of Greek cookery, lends its unique fruity taste. A symbol of the Mediterranean, the olive tree is famous for its outstandingly long life. Olives are picked by hand then taken in crates or bags to be pressed. Stripped of their leaves and tailed, they are washed then crushed. The resulting pulp is spread into 1-inch/2.5-centimeter deep layers on the disks of a hydraulic press.

The resulting liquid is next put into a centrifuge that separates the oil from the water. The oil is then stored away from the light in terracotta jars or steel tanks. In Greece, the area around Kalloni in Attica has been renowned for thousands of years for the excellence and jewel-like color of its oil.

In this recipe, the chicken is served with *chilopites*. These little pasta shapes are usually home made and come in many different varieties. Cooked with the tomatoes, they can be replaced with any pasta shape you like.

Before serving the *chilopites* don't forget to scatter some *myzithra* over the top. This slightly salty cheese, similar to Italian Pecorino has been made in Greece for thousands of years. Originally from Macedonia, it is also known as *manouri* in Epirus and *ourda* or *anthotiros* in Crete.

With a sharp knife joint the chicken, separating the breast, legs and wings.

In a large pan, heat the olive oil and brown the diced onion. Add the chicken pieces and brown for about 5 minutes.

Pour on the white wine and leave to reduce for about 5 minutes.

Chilopites

Add the bay leaf and the cinnamon stick to the pan with the chicken, then the peeled and chopped tomatoes and cook for about 5 minutes.

Add just enough water to cover the chicken, season and cook for about 1½ hours, adding more water if necessary.

Add the chilopites and cook for about 2 minutes. Divide the chicken and noodles between 4 plates and top with the grated cheese.

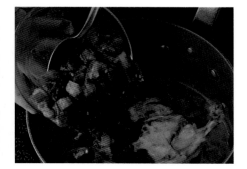

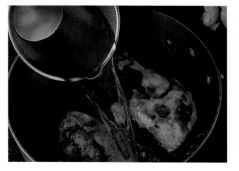

Giouvetsi

Preparation time: 35 minutes
Cooking time: 1 hour
Difficulty: ☆

Serves 4

1¾ lb/800 g	shoulder of veal
6	tomatoes
5–6 tbsp	olive oil
1	meat bouillon cube
3–4 tbsp	white wine
3	bay leaves
6	allspice berries
2	onions
	salt
10 oz/300 g	chilopites (Greek pasta)
1½ tbsp	grated Pecorino cheese

The word *giouvetsi* comes from the name of the earthenware dish in which meat was left to simmer in times gone by. A very popular dish in major Greek cities, this veal stew is enriched with *chilopites*, handmade pasta shapes. This tasty dish can be enjoyed on any occasion.

Greek cuisine traditionally does not use much veal. In this Mediterranean country the scrubland has left its wild imprint on the landscape and has gradually eroded the meadowland. As a result, since the days of Ancient Greece the locals have preferred to eat lamb and mutton.

In olden days cattle were raised for the sole purpose of helping man to work in the fields. Only an animal that had been blessed could be killed and eaten. According to Nicolaos Katsanis, the villagers would club together and buy the meat from the owner in order that he could purchase another animal.

This recipe allows the delicate flavor of the shoulder of veal to emerge, a meat appreciated for its delicacy and smoothness.

Simmered with olive oil, onions, white wine, and tomatoes, it is further enhanced with the distinctive flavor of bay leaf. Known as *dafni* in Greek, this plant owes its name to the pretty nymph Daphne. According to mythology, Daphne was changed into a laurel bush by the gods of Olympus to help her escape the unwanted attentions of the handsome Apollo. Used whole or crumbled, the leaves of this bush are used sparingly. They give an admirable lift to stews, stuffing mixes, and marinades.

Served with pasta shapes, *giouvetsi* is a filling dish. If you have difficulty finding *chilopites* you can use macaroni. Depending on your personal taste, you can also try this recipe with pork without compromising the finished result.

Using a sharp knife, trim the shoulder of veal and cut the meat into cubes of equal thickness. Cut one tomato into thin slices and set aside. Peel and chop the rest.

Heat 4 tbsp olive oil in a pan and add the cubes of veal. Brown them quickly over a high heat for a couple of minutes. Crumble the meat bouillon cube into a cup of water and set aside.

Add the white wine to the veal, 2 bay leaves, 3 allspice berries, and the prepared stock. Top up with water to cover the meat. Cook for 35–40 minutes.

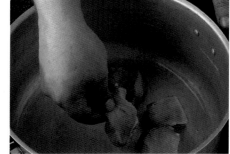

Heat the remaining olive oil in a deep pan and brown the diced onions. Add the chopped tomatoes, remaining allspice berries, and bay leaf. Cook for 10 minutes. Transfer the meat and the stock it was cooked in to the tomato mixture. Season with salt and cook for 10 minutes.

Bring a pan of salted water to the boil and add the chilopites. Cook for about 3 minutes then drain.

Transfer the meat mixture to an earthenware dish and add the chilopites. Top with the reserved tomato slices. Cook in an oven preheated to 350° F/180° C for 20 minutes. Serve the giouvetsi scattered with grated Pecorino.

Dried Beans with

Preparation time:	30 minutes
Cooking time:	2 hours
	40 minutes
Soaking time (beans):	overnight
Difficulty:	★★

Serves 6

2½ cups/500 g	large dried lima beans (large white beans)
3½ oz/100 g	leek
2 stalks	celery
3½ oz/100 g	carrots
7 oz/200 g	Mani sausages

2 or 3	scallions
1¾ cups/400 ml	extra-virgin olive oil
2½ cups/600 ml	tomato juice
2	bay leaves
	salt
	paprika
	dill

Miltos Karoubas found the recipe for this rich gratin of dried white beans in the Mani area of the Peloponnese. Locally produced sausages lend their characteristic smoky flavor enhanced by orange zest.

Since the days of Ancient Greece and the Byzantines, dried beans have provided a rich source of nourishment for even the poorest Greek families, whether in soups, stews, or gratins. The large variety that we are going to use in this recipe are known as *gigantes* in Greek, some of the beans weighing as much as a quarter of an ounce/eight grams. Cooks particularly appreciate comforting dishes like this in the winter. Today most of the giant dried white beans grown in Greece come from Florina in western Macedonia.

It is the delicious sausages that make this dish such a winner. Mani sausages are made from a mix of finely chopped pork meat and pork fat, different spices, and finely grated orange peel which is stuffed into a tube of pig intestine. They are then hung up to dry before being smoked. Between 15 and 20 inches long/40–50 centimeters, they are orangey brown on the outside and light pink on the inside. They are stored in the open, although on some islands they are smeared with fat and stored in terracotta pots.

Throughout Greece you can find other specialty sausages flavored with orange, particularly in Trikala, Ionnina, Skyros, Andros, Tinos, and on Crete. In other areas the same dish is made with bacon or small pieces of pork instead of the sausages.

First brown the sausages with the onion and leek and then add the beans (already cooked and soft) to the fat released from the sausages. Once the tomatoes and spices have been added, enhance the dish by topping it with breadcrumbs and grated cheese and cook it in the oven for a long time.

Soak the beans in water overnight. Drain and boil in a pan of salted water for 1½ hours or until they are soft.

Chop the white part of the leek. Finely slice the stalks of celery and the peeled carrots.

Slice the sausages.

Mani Sausages

In a large pan, brown chopped scallions with the sausages and leek in olive oil, then add the cooked beans. Stir rapidly.

Add the carrots and celery and leave to simmer for 5–6 minutes over a fairly high heat.

Finally add the tomato juice, bay leaves, salt, pinch of paprika, and just enough water to just cover. Bring to the boil then transfer to an ovenproof dish and cook for 50 minutes in an oven preheated to 350° F/180° C. Scatter with chopped dill and serve piping hot.

Lamb Shanks with

Preparation time: 45 minutes
Cooking time: 45 minutes
Difficulty: ★

Serves 4

1½ tbsp	olive oil
2	onions
1 clove	garlic
4	lamb shanks
	salt
	pepper
12 oz/350 g	tomatoes
1 sprig	thyme
2	bay leaves
2 tbsp	red wine

For the eggplant caviar:

8	eggplants
	salt
	pepper
2 tbsp	olive oil
1	onion
scant ½ cup/ 50 g	all-purpose flour
⅓ cup/80 ml	warm milk
	nutmeg
½ cup/70 g	grated *kefalotyri* cheese
1 bunch	parsley

For the garnish:

	bay leaf

An extremely popular dish in northern Greece, lamb shanks with eggplant caviar is a real delight. A fairly filling dish, it is most often served in winter.

In this wonderful country with its strong pastoral tradition, lamb is eaten in lots of different ways. Full of flavor, it is often broiled on a spit or on skewers but can also be made into stews. In this recipe, the lamb is combined with the aromas of thyme, bay leaf, garlic, onion, and red wine. When baked in the oven for about 40 minutes, these ingredients meld together and the resultant dish is simply bursting with the flavors of local produce. Our chef suggests you also try this recipe with whole leg or shoulder of lamb.

A typical item in the Greek culinary repertoire, eggplant caviar is made according to family or regional recipes, so there are lots of variations. It is a very popular dish and can be eaten on any occasion. It sometimes finds its way into the array of Greek appetizers known as *mezze* but can also be served with a range of different meat dishes. Panagiotis Delvenakiotis suggests enriching it with a béchamel sauce.

Particularly rich and smooth, eggplant caviar is embellished with the warm sweet flavor of nutmeg. Native to the Spice Islands it is often used to flavor milk-based dishes. The nutmeg itself is oval in shape, the size of an almond, dark grayish-brown and is always used finely grated. It should be stored in an airtight glass container.

To accentuate the Greek origins of this dish, our chef is cooking the eggplants with *kefalotyri*, a cheese made from ewe's milk and goat's milk. Originally produced in the mountainous part of the country, it comes into its own when used as an accompaniment to pasta and in pie fillings. If you can't find *kefalotyri*, use Gruyère instead. Tasty in the extreme, try this family dish for yourself today.

Heat the olive oil in a metal roasting pan and brown 2 chopped onions and a crushed clove of garlic. Season the pieces of meat and brown them in the pan.

Add tomatoes cut into chunks to the pan, cook for about 3 minutes, then add the thyme and bay leaves.

Add the red wine. Cover the pan with a sheet of foil and cook for 15 minutes. Transfer the pan to an oven preheated to 340° F/180° C for about 40 minutes.

Eggplant Caviar

Prick the eggplant skins and broil them for about 35 minutes. Peel, and put the flesh into a bowl. Season, add 1 tbsp olive oil, and mash it all together.

To make the béchamel sauce, add the rest of the olive oil to a clean pan. Fry the diced onion until it just changes color, add the flour, and stir briskly with a wooden spoon. Add the milk, a little grated nutmeg, and stir until thickened.

Transfer the eggplant purée into the béchamel sauce, mix thoroughly and cook for 3 minutes. Scatter with the cheese and chopped parsley. Serve the lamb and tomatoes with the eggplant, garnished with a bay leaf.

Kleftiko

Preparation time:	35 minutes
Cooking time:	1 hour
Difficulty:	★

Serves 4

1¾ lb/800 g	shoulder of lamb
2	tomatoes
2	zucchini
2	green bell peppers
2	pearl onions
2	small potatoes
4 cloves	garlic

1 bunch	mint
1 tbsp	olive oil (optional)
5½ oz/150 g	feta cheese
	salt
	pepper
1 tsp	dried oregano

For the garnish (optional):

| | grape (vine) leaves |
| | oregano sprigs |

Kleftiko, which in Greek literally means "thief's meat" is a classic in the country's culinary repertoire. An extremely popular dish, it originated in Thessalia and is primarily served as a Sunday family meal.

Kleftiko dates back to the Ottoman period and is unlike any other dish as it has very close associations with the country's history. It became a symbol of the resistance of a whole people and is surrounded by legend, passed down in witness of the bravery of past generations of Greeks.

According to our chef, "thief's meat" owes its name to some shepherds who were fighting for the independence of their country. The shepherds would split up into two groups. The first group would go down into the valley and rustle a sheep, while the second group would use different stratagems to build an underground oven and get a fire going. Once prepared, the animal's belly would be stuffed with vegetables then sewn up again and the carcass roasted over the fire, an operation conducted in the utmost secrecy!

Even having made such a famous name for itself, *kleftiko* is still firmly rooted in the countryside. Encased in sheets of waxed paper, or even pastry in some areas, the flavors of the ingredients fuse with one another and are impregnated with the flavors of the mint and oregano.

Wonderfully bright to look at, this special dish also includes vegetables from the kitchen garden. Zucchini, tomatoes, potatoes, and onions are served around the lamb. And when they're in season, you could add some peas too.

Typically Greek in its flavors, this recipe is enhanced with the salty taste of the feta, which was already being produced in Ancient Greece. Hippocrates, the father of medicine, used to recommend it for its nutritional virtues.

Using a cleaver, cut the shoulder of lamb into 4 thick slices, then use a knife to trim them so they are all the same size.

Wash the tomatoes, zucchini, and bell peppers and peel the pearl onions and potatoes. Remove the seeds and the white membrane from the peppers and cut all of the vegetables into big cubes.

Peel the cloves of garlic and cut them into slivers. Wash the mint and strip the leaves from the stalks.

Lay a sheet of waxed paper on top of the work board. Add 1 slice meat and an assortment of different vegetables. Drizzle with some olive oil if the meat does not already have some fat.

Scatter the mint leaves and cubes of feta around the meat, season, and sprinkle with oregano. Repeat with the other 3 pieces of meat.

Fold the paper around the meat so it is entirely encased. Wrap each parcel in a sheet of foil, and cook on a baking sheet in an oven preheated to 350° F/180° C for about 2 hours. Open the parcels and serve the contents on the washed/steamed grape leaves with oregano.

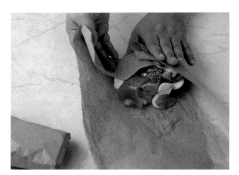

Moussaka

Preparation time: 45 minutes
Cooking time: 1 hour 30 minutes
Sweating time (eggplants): 30 minutes
Difficulty: ★★

Serves 4

3½ lb/1.5 kg	ripe eggplants
	salt
	olive oil
1	large red onion
1¼ lb/ 550 g	ground lamb
4 tbsp	virgin olive oil
1 stick	cinnamon

1 pinch	nutmeg
1 cup/250 ml	tomato juice
	pepper
2 cups/100 g	breadcrumbs

For the béchamel sauce:

2 oz/55 g	butter
½ cup 60 g	all-purpose flour
2 cups/500 ml	milk
	salt
	pepper
1 pinch	nutmeg
2	eggs
2 tbsp	grated parmesan

A Greek dish that is now internationally known and loved, moussaka can be traced as far afield as the Middle East and Iran. The origin of the name is not known, but a virtually identical recipe is shared by Greeks, Turks, Iranians, and their neighbors. The Greek version, though, has only been smothered in a layer of béchamel sauce for the past 90 or 100 years. Before that, cooks would arrange the layers of tomatoes or eggplants on the bed of meat to prevent it from drying out during cooking. In Greek families, moussaka is usually eaten as a main course, although some restaurant owners, who really have tried making it in many different ways, have been serving it as an appetizer for the past 20 years or so.

You can sprinkle the slices of eggplant with salt and wait until they "sweat," in other words until their somewhat bitter juice forms into droplets on the surface of the cut slices. Then rinse them under cold running water and blot dry.

When they are fried, don't forget to blot them again on kitchen paper to soak up the excess oil (for maximum drainage, our chef recommends you do this the night before). If you put a bed of breadcrumbs on the bottom of the gratin dish this will also soak up the oil.

Moussaka is usually made with lamb, although some Greeks prefer to use mutton. In fact in the countryside, some lambs weigh up to 12–15 pounds/5–7 kilograms. Greek cooks prefer to bake their tender flesh, essentially the leg and shoulder, in the oven with potatoes.

Moussaka comes in many different varieties, according to the cook's mood. You can add slices of potato or fried zucchini. Our chef sometimes cuts the meat into fine strips and alternates it with mushrooms. It is even possible to replace lamb with beef. Just before serving, cut the moussaka into portions and garnish with the green parts of the scallions.

Cut the eggplants into slices, put them in a colander, sprinkle with salt, and leave for 30 minutes. Blot dry and fry in olive oil until brown.

In another skillet fry the chopped onion and meat in 4 tbsp olive oil over a fairly brisk heat for 10–15 minutes, breaking the meat up with a fork until it has a uniform consistency.

Stir in the cinnamon stick, nutmeg, tomato juice, salt, and pepper. Add water just to cover the contents and continue cooking over a brisk heat for 10 minutes or until the liquid has evaporated.

For the béchamel sauce: Melt the butter and stir in the flour until it forms a roux. Whisk in the milk and continue whisking over low heat to achieve a thick, smooth sauce. Add seasoning, and nutmeg.

In a separate bowl, whisk the eggs. Take the béchamel off the heat and beat in the eggs, together with the grated cheese. Adjust the seasoning.

Oil a gratin dish and sprinkle in half the breadcrumbs. Layer the eggplants and meat, cover with béchamel sauce, and the remaining breadcrumbs. Cook for 50 minutes in an oven preheated to 400° F/200° C.

Lachanosarmades

Preparation time:	*40 minutes*	
Cooking time:	*55 minutes*	
Difficulty:	*	

Serves 4

1	large white cabbage
1	meat bouillon cube
5 tbsp	olive oil
	salt

For the stuffing:

1 lb/450 g	ground pork
1 lb/450 g	ground beef
3	onions
3	scallions
1 bunch	parsley
scant ½ cup/85 g	Arborio rice
1 pinch	boukovo (dried flakes of red pimento)
	salt
	pepper
1	egg

For the avgolemono sauce:

1 tbsp	cornstarch
1	lemon
2	egg yolks
	salt
	pepper

For the garnish:

	lemon zest
	boukovo

A very popular dish throughout the whole of Greece, these stuffed, rolled cabbage leaves, known as *lachanosarmades* or even *lachanodolmades*, are particularly popular in winter. Originally from the town of Kozani in the north of the country, this adaptation is full of incomparable flavors.

Highly regarded in both Greek and Turkish cooking, the cabbage has been known in Europe for more than 4,000 years. Cabbage production spread across the whole of the continent during the Middle Ages. Rich in vitamins A and C, it has a fairly sweet taste. Choose a white cabbage that is a hard, densely packed ball, free of blemishes. If you want to make this recipe with a savoy cabbage instead, because the leaves have an embossed texture, you will need to keep a close watch on it while it is cooking. Rolled into cigar shapes, the leaves should not start to unravel when they are being cooked. Our chef recommends that you wedge them firmly into the dish by putting a plate on top of them.

Greeks love vegetables and have poured all their talents into the art of cooking them: Fried, broiled, puréed, they are also very often served stuffed. In this recipe, the beef and pork used for the filling are combined with onions, parsley, eggs … and rice.

Eaten now throughout the whole world, rice was first imported to Ancient Greece via Mesopotamia and the Persians, and reached Greece in the 4th century B.C. when Alexander the Great introduced it to the country. Initially regarded as a luxury, rice is today part of the staple diet.

These succulent *lachanosarmades* are coated at the last minute with an *avgolemono* sauce, which is made from eggs, lemon juice, stock, cornstarch, salt, and pepper. It provides a lift to many dishes, and is served in generous portions. It is vital that you use a whisk when you are making it to ensure all the ingredients are thoroughly blended.

Use a sharp knife to remove the tough cabbage stalk. Plunge the trimmed cabbage head into a large pan of boiling salted water and let it blanch for about 10 minutes.

Drain and cool the cabbage, then using your fingers tease apart the leaves. Make up the stock with the bouillon cube and set it aside.

For the stuffing: Mix the two meats, chopped onions and scallions, chopped parsley, and rice. Sprinkle on the boukovo, salt, and pepper, add the egg, and stir well.

Cut away the central rib from the cabbage leaves and cut the leaves in half, if large. Add the stuffing, fold in the sides and roll up firmly.

Line the bottom of a deep skillet with some cabbage leaves, and put the rolls on top, wedging them in. Cover with more leaves. Add the stock and olive oil. Cover and cook over moderate heat for about 45 minutes. Pour off the cooking liquid into a bowl.

Pour half of the partially cooled cooking liquid into a pan. Whisk in the cornstarch and lemon juice. Now add the remaining cooking liquid and egg yolks. Season, and pour over the rolls. Garnish with lemon zest and boukovo.

Rabbit with

Preparation time:	35 minutes
Cooking time:	35 minutes
Marinating time (rabbit):	5 hours
Difficulty:	★

Serves 4

1	rabbit weighing 3 lb/1.4 kg
3–4 tbsp	olive oil
10–12	pearl onions
1 clove	garlic
	salt
	pepper

scant ½ cup/ 100 ml	vegetable stock
1¼ lb/550 g	green olives, pitted

For the marinade:

2 cloves	garlic
1 sprig	thyme
2 sprigs	rosemary
2	bay leaves
1 stalk	celery
½	onion
⅔ cup/150 ml	red wine

For the garnish:

	rosemary

Rabbit with green olives is a specialty from Chalkidiki. Forming an enormous peninsula in the shape of a foot from which three "toes" jut out into the Aegean Sea, this hunting and fishing area of northeastern Greece is famous for its traditional cuisine. This exquisite family dish can be enjoyed on any occasion.

In the Greek culinary repertoire, rabbit is a particularly popular meat. It is usually cooked in olive oil with vegetables, which make the perfect foil. In this recipe the firm flesh of the rabbit takes up the flavors of the marinade. If you can, use a short stocky rabbit, with a plump saddle and a pale, unblemished liver. During the hunting season, rabbit can be easily be replaced by hare or wild rabbit.

A mirror image of the landscapes in the Greek hinterland, this dish is a marvelous melting pot for a range of different aromas. Always used very sparingly, thyme, bay leaf, and rosemary really complement the wine used to marinade the meat. Celery, or *selino* as it is known in Greece, grows wild here and is similar to flat-leaf parsley. It has a very distinctive taste that is also popular in soups and stews.

Wonderfully colorful, this dish confirms its Mediterranean origins thanks to the use of green olives. As Greek as Greece itself, these fruits of the olive tree originally came from the Orient. Recognizable by their oval shape, the generous flesh encases a torpedo shaped stone. They are used for the production of olive oil and as a table condiment.

Picked before they are fully ripe from mid September to the end of November, green olives are then preserved in oil or brine. The olives grown in Chalkidiki are quite big and are often stuffed with walnuts, almonds or peppers.

Remove the liver from the rabbit and split the chest cage from stem to stern at the junction of the ribs and saddle. Pull off the legs and cut them up. Divide the saddle into equal pieces.

For the marinade: Put the crushed cloves of garlic, thyme, rosemary, bay leaves, celery, and the chopped onion into a bowl. Add the pieces of rabbit, pour over the red wine, and set aside for 5 hours.

Heat the olive oil in a pan and brown the rabbit pieces. Add the thyme, the bay leaf from the marinade, the peeled pearl onions, 1 crushed clove of garlic and some seasoning.

Green Olives

Add the wine from the strained marinade to the rabbit. Cook for 5 minutes, add a scant ½ cup/100 ml vegetable stock and cook for 20–25 minutes.

Add the olives to the rabbit. Cook for 3 minutes, then lift out the olives, pearl onions and the meat.

Strain the sauce. Serve the rabbit with the green olives and pearl onions. Pour over the sauce and garnish with rosemary.

Chios Rabbit and

Preparation time:	*35 minutes*
Cooking time:	*45 minutes*
Marinating time (rabbit):	*12 hours*
Difficulty:	✶

Serves 4

1	rabbit weighing 3 lb/1.4 kg
3 tbsp	olive oil
5	scallions
2¼ lb/1 kg	tomatoes
3½ lb/1.5 kg	wild green leaves (dandelion, chicory)

5	mastic leaves (see below)
3	bay leaves
	salt

For the marinade:

1	onion
3 cloves	garlic
scant ½ cup/ 100 ml	red wine
3–4 tbsp	olive oil

In the little villages to the north of the island of Chios, hunting is an ancestral activity. In winter, families like to gather round the table to eat the game brought home by the hunters. Rabbit with wild vegetables is a typical dish from this lovely region.

Easy to make, this rustic dish is a wonderful concoction of different flavors. Left to marinate for about 12 hours in red wine, garlic, onion, and olive oil, the meat of the rabbit not only becomes more tender, it is also impregnated with all the aromas in the marinade. Choose a young, full-bodied red wine if you can. Another word of advice: Stir the marinade with a wooden spoon every three hours.

Greatly prized in Greek cooking, rabbit is popular for its dense and flavorsome meat. Available all year long on market stalls, it should have a plump saddle and a pale, blemish-free liver. Be careful when cooking it, as rabbit can dry out. During the hunting season, you could replace it with hare or wild rabbit – the result will be just as delicious.

In Chios the villagers use a lot of wild leaves in their cooking. But these can be replaced by dandelion, chicory, or even young spinach shoots – whatever you can obtain.

On this island, which according to one legend was the birthplace of Homer, there is a wonderful tree called the mastic or lentisc tree. An evergreen, it grows to 6–10 feet/2–3 meters and its resin is used to produce a very popular chewing gum that is eaten all over Greece and Turkey. In this recipe the leaves of the mastic tree lend their own particular aroma and our chef says they are irreplaceable. However, rosemary might do!

Wonderfully aromatic, rabbit with wild vegetables from Chios is a dish to be discovered without further delay.

Remove the liver of the rabbit, split the chest cage from stem to stern at the junction of the ribs and the saddle. Pull off the legs and cut them up. Divide the saddle into equal pieces.

For the marinade: Chop the onion, peel the cloves of garlic and put in a bowl with the rabbit pieces. Stir in the red wine and olive oil and marinate for 12 hours. Strain and reserve the liquid and the garlic cloves.

Heat 3 tbsp olive oil and brown the rabbit and then the chopped scallions. Add the cloves of garlic from the marinade.

Wild Vegetables

Add the marinade liquid to the pan containing the rabbit. Cook for about 5 minutes, add chopped tomatoes, and cook for 15 minutes. Remove the rabbit and reserve the cooking juices.

Wash the wild leaves and blanch them for 2 minutes in boiling water, then drain. Put the rabbit pieces into a roasting pan and add the wild leaves.

Put the mastic leaves, or rosemary sprigs, and the bay leaves on top, pour over the cooking juices from the rabbit, season with salt, and cook in an oven preheated to 400° F/200° C for about 20 minutes.

Rabbit with Langoustines

Preparation time: 50 minutes
Cooking time: 1 hour
Difficulty: ★★

Serves 4

4	rabbit thighs
1	carrot
1 stalk	celery
2	onions
	salt
	pepper
3–4 tbsp	olive oil
1½ tbsp	*babatzim* (spirit)
2	tomatoes

1 generous cup/ 200 g	brown lentils
½ bunch	parsley

For the stuffing:

3½ oz/100 g	rabbit meat (scraped from the rib cage etc.)
2 oz/55 g	button mushrooms
	salt
	pepper
1½ tbsp	*babatzim* (spirit)
1	egg white
8	langoustines

For the garnish:

	thyme

Nikos Sarandos has adapted this dish of rabbit stuffed with langoustines flavored with *babatzim* from a traditional recipe from Kynouria in the Peloponnese. The cuisine from this region is characterized by its very rich recipes based on game and carbohydrates. In this dish our chef has brought together produce from the sea and the mountains with a degree of flair that makes it a real triumph.

Greeks love rabbit for its lean and strongly flavored meat. Choose one that is compact, with a plump saddle and a pale, unblemished liver. During the hunting season you could also use wild rabbit, which is equally delicious.

In this country, the sea, which bathes the little groups of islands in a vivid turquoise, has always shared its bounty with the inhabitants. In creating this dish, Nikos Sarandos pays homage to the sea. Sought after for their delicate flavor, which is similar to that of lobster, the langoustines

absorb the aroma of the *babatzim*, a grape-based spirit. They can be found on fishmongers' stalls all year round, and are rich in calcium, phosphorus, and iron. When you buy them they should still be whole and have their pincers, and their shells should be bright and shiny. They can be replaced by shrimp.

Synonymous with Greek cooking, lentils are usually served with meat. Eaten for thousands of years, these pulses originated in the East. According to documents dating back to Ancient Greece, Athenians from the century of Pericles used to eat them with every meal. Unlike garbanzo beans, they do not need soaking.

Perfumed with the olive oil and cooked with onions, tomatoes, and parsley, the lentils add great finesse and magnify the flavors of the stuffed rabbit.

Using a knife, completely bone the rabbit thighs, starting at the tip. Reserve the bones. Prepare a stock by cooking the bones for 20 minutes in a large pan filled with water, to which the peeled and roughly chopped carrot, celery, and 1 onion have been added.

For the stuffing: Put the rabbit meat into a bowl with the peeled and finely diced mushrooms. Season, then stir in the babatzim and egg white.

Fill the boned rabbit thighs with the stuffing mixture. Shell the langoustines and put 2 into each thigh.

Flavored with Babatzim

Carefully close up each thigh using wooden toothpicks. Season. Strain the stock.

Brown the rabbit thighs in 1½ tbsp olive oil. Add the babatzim. Leave to reduce slightly, add the strained stock, and transfer to a roasting pan. Cook in an oven preheated to 350° F/180° C for about 30 minutes.

Brown the second chopped onion in the remaining olive oil and add the tomatoes. Add the lentils, water, if necessary, and cook for 40 minutes. Add chopped parsley and season. Serve garnished with thyme.

Rabbit

Preparation time:	45 minutes		1	leek
Cooking time:	1 hour		½ cup/125 ml	olive oil
	35 minutes		1	cinnamon stick
Difficulty:	★★		3 or 4	cloves
			4 or 5	allspice berries
Serves 6				salt
				pepper
1	rabbit weighing 3½ lb/		4 tbsp	red wine vinegar
	1.5 kg, skinned		½ cup/125 ml	red *brusco* wine
	and cleaned		2 cloves	garlic
3 cups/300 g	cauliflower florets		2	bay leaves
1¼ lb/600 g	pearl onions		1 sprig	rosemary
7 oz/200 g	oyster mushrooms		8	small plum tomatoes
5 oz/150 g	carrots			

Braised rabbit, or *lagos stifado* is traditionally simmered in the middle of an assortment of fresh colourful vegetables and is always rightfully appreciated on Greek tables. Characteristic of many local dishes, the abundance of vegetables and herbs gives this recipe its individual flavor.

In the mountainous and arid country that is Greece, the inhabitants generally eat only a little meat from farmed animals (lamb, goat, rabbit) or game (hare, partridge, etc). Ask your butcher to prepare the rabbit or choose prepacked ones that are ready to cook. This recipe is equally good when made with hare, lamb, or beef.

When garnishing the dish, oyster mushrooms can be easily replaced by stronger-flavored wild ones or even button mushrooms. *Brusco* is a sweet and delicate red wine from Patras in the Peloponnese.

Our chef usually adds a few sun-ripened Greek baby tomatoes, which are very tasty, and much prefers these to the sort of insipid tomatoes that are grown under glass. But if you can't find these, choose small plum tomatoes instead, or even peeled tinned ones. Tomatoes are yet another vegetable introduced relatively recently to Greece. Brought back from the Americas in the 16th century by Portuguese sailors, it would be a couple of centuries before they were grown in Hellenic gardens.

If you need to cook the dish quickly, you can put all the ingredients into an oiled heavy-bottomed pan and cook it on top of the stove. For a better flavor and color, though, it's best to first fry the rabbit with the mushrooms, carrots, leek, onions, and the seasoning (cinnamon, cloves, allspice, and garlic). Pour on the wine and vinegar, then add the other vegetables and herbs and braise the dish in the oven.

Cut the rabbit into 3 large pieces, then cut it again into pieces of about 3–4 in/8–10 cm.

Blanch the cauliflower florets and refresh. Peel the onions. Cut the mushrooms into big pieces, peel the carrots and slice thinly. Trim and wash the leek, slice into thin rings.

Heat a little oil in a heavy-bottomed casserole dish and sauté the rabbit, mushrooms, carrots, pearl onions, leeks, cinnamon stick, cloves, allspice berries, salt and pepper.

Stifado

Pour the vinegar and red wine over the rabbit and vegetables and mix well.

Add peeled garlic, bay leaves, rosemary, and chopped tomatoes.

Add the cauliflower florets to the casserole. Cover and braise in a moderate oven for 1½ hours, adding water if necessary.

Macedonian

Preparation time: 20 minutes
Cooking time: 40 minutes
Difficulty: ☆

Serves 4

1¾ lb/800 g	blade shoulder of pork
3–4 tbsp	olive oil
16	pearl onions
3–4 tbsp	white wine
7 oz/200 g	tomatoes
1 stick	cinnamon

	pepper
4	quinces
1	lemon
2 tbsp	vegetable oil
16	cloves
12	prunes
	salt

This pork dish is an extremely refined, marvelous amalgamation of sweet and slightly sharp flavors. This recipe has been around for centuries, dating as far back as the Eastern Roman Empire, and has been passed down from generation to generation ever since. A splendid example of Byzantine culinary refinements, this traditional Macedonian dish uses blade shoulder (chine) of pork with a mix of fresh and dried fruits to great effect.

Enriched with a caramel sauce in some parts of Greece, Macedonian pork is usually made in the fall when quinces are in season. Symbols of fecundity in Ancient Greece, quinces are associated with Aphrodite, the goddess of love. In the days of Pericles they were cooked with honey and encased in pastry. These days the best quinces come from Kydonia on Crete. Originally from Iran and the Caucasus, these fruits of the japonica bush are pale yellow and round in shape. They are hard and sharp-flavored so cannot be eaten raw, but once cooked they become sweet and lose a lot of their sharpness. Nicolaos Katsanis suggests you sometimes ring the changes and use potatoes for this recipe, but advises you add the juice of a lemon if you do.

This ancient recipe also uses prunes from Skopelos in Thessalia. Made from damson plums, which are always picked in August, the fruit is laid out on a pallet and left to dry in the sun for about three weeks before being put into a cool oven overnight to finish drying them. The resulting oblong, particularly sharp, dark purple prunes are often used in Greek cookery. They have a lemony taste and are used to great effect in savory dishes. Rich in vitamins A and B, they do not need to be soaked. You could also use dark red plums instead.

Use a knife to trim the pork and cut it into equal slices.

Put the olive oil into a big pan, add the peeled pearl onions and the pork and fry until brown. Add the white wine, reduce the glaze a little then cook for 5 minutes.

Add chopped tomatoes to the pan plus ¾ cup/200 ml water. Cook for 5 minutes, add the cinnamon stick and pepper and cook for another 10 minutes.

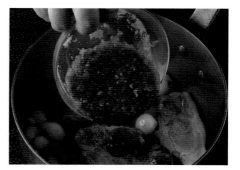

Pork

Peel the quinces with a potato peeler, remove the seeds, and cut into quarters. Put in a bowl of water with some slices of lemon.

Drain the quinces, transfer to a skillet and brown them in the vegetable oil. Drain on paper towels, stud with cloves, and add to the pan with the meat.

Add the prunes and some salt. Cook over a gentle heat for about 15 minutes. Divide the pork between 4 plates and drizzle some sauce around the meat and fruit.

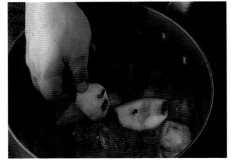

Yiaourtlou

Preparation time: 35 minutes
Cooking time: 20 minutes
Rehydration time (raisins): 10 minutes
Difficulty: ★

Serves 4

1¼ lb/600 g	pork fillet
	salt, pepper

For the yiaourtlou:

3 cloves	garlic
1	onion
3–4 tbsp	olive oil
10 oz/300 g	peeled tomatoes
	salt, pepper
1 tsp	cumin
3 tsp	dried cilantro
1 tsp	boukovo (flaked dried pimento)

¾ cup/150 g	Greek, or thick creamy, yogurt

For the pilau:

2 tbsp	raisins
2 tbsp each	brandy, olive oil
3	small onions
1	leek
	salt, pepper
½ cup/100 g	Arborio rice
3–4 tbsp	white wine
1	lemon
2 tbsp	toasted pine nuts
4 sprigs	dill

For the garnish:

	dill

This ancient recipe has its roots firmly planted on the banks of the Bosphorus and illustrates the flair and refinement of the cuisine of Constantinople. Its wonderful Eastern flavors make it an enchanting experience for the taste buds.

In this recipe our chef wanted to pay homage to Jean Moshos, a monk and great traveler who crossed the known world in the 6th century A.D. Starting from Mount Athos with the goal of reaching the Sudan, this man of the church crossed Libya, Syria, and Egypt. During the course of his odyssey he discovered a range of precious spices. A deeply erudite man, he recorded his experiences in a book of recipes entitled *Spiritual Valleys*.

This cookery book is full of anecdotes and offers a wonderful insight into the tastes of people living at that time. Among the recipes he brought back with him was one for a pilau, a dish that was very popular in Constantinople.

Aristedes Pasparakis has used exactly the same ingredients here, but has combined the pilau with pork *yiaourtlou*.

This dish is made extra special by its use of spices and aromatic herbs. This pilau, a rice-based preparation, uses dill that releases its own particular sweet, aniseed flavor. Dill grows wild all around the Mediterranean basin, and was valued in Ancient Greece for its digestive and stimulating properties. In Greece, as well as in Turkey, it is used to give a lift to dishes made from fish or dairy products.

The *yiaourtlou* sauce, meanwhile, is made with Greek yogurt. The pork is added to the sauce, which is redolent of Eastern flavors, including dried cilantro and cumin, which are given the chance of expressing themselves to the full.

Use a sharp knife to cut the pork into equal sized medallions. Soak the raisins in the brandy for 10 minutes to rehydrate them.

For the pilau: Trim the small onions and leek and chop finely. Fry in the olive oil, season, stir in the rice. Add the white wine and cook until the liquid has evaporated.

Add lemon peel, and the raisins in brandy. Cook for 5 minutes then add the pine nuts, chopped dill, and lemon juice. Cover with water and cook for 10 minutes. Season.

Pork

To make the yiaourtlou sauce: Fry chopped garlic and onion in olive oil. Add the peeled tomatoes and cook for about 10 minutes. Season, then stir in the cumin, cilantro, and boukovo.

Take the pan off the heat and add the Greek yogurt. Stir gently and set aside.

Season the medallions of pork and dry-fry in a nonstick skillet. Arrange them on 4 plates with the pilau and yiaourtlou sauce, garnished with dill.

Greek-style

Preparation time: 1 hour
Cooking time: 45 minutes
Difficulty: ★★★

Serves 4

1	chicken weighing
	4½–5½ lb/2–2.5 kg
	salt
1	carrot
1 stick	celery
3 cloves	garlic
1	onion
1	potato
½	leek
4 tbsp	olive oil
3–4 tbsp	red wine
2	tomatoes

For the stuffing:

5	scallions
4 tbsp	olive oil
½ cup/100 g	yellow rice
1 clove	garlic
3–4 tbsp	white wine
1 lb/450 g	peeled chestnuts
½ cup/60 g	pine nuts
½ cup/50 g	raisins
1	apple
1 sprig	oregano
	salt

For the sauce:

2 tbsp	sugar
½	lemon
1 tsp	cornstarch

This extremely elegant Greek-style stuffed chicken is usually served as part of the New Year celebrations. Its sweet-salty flavors make this dish a real joy for the taste buds.

Prized for its firm meat, chicken needs a longer cooking time. Our chef recommends that after stuffing it, you insert the pulp from a lemon into the cavity before baking it. And when you come to deglaze the pan with the red wine, don't forget to sprinkle a little water over the chicken so that it doesn't burn or dry out too much. Then cover the dish with sheets of cooking foil. If you prefer you can use turkey instead for this recipe.

The extremely rich stuffing is made from rice, apple, pine nuts and is a classic in the Greek culinary repertoire. Chestnuts go wonderfully well with poultry. They are very filling and highly prized for their delicate taste. If you want to use fresh chestnuts instead, cut a cross on the base with a sharp knife then plunge them into boiling water that will enable you to peel them more easily.

The stuffing mixture also uses Corinthian raisins from the Ionian islands. They have a distinctive taste and dark color, and are sold with their seeds removed. They come from a very sweet grape variety and are dried either in the sun or artificially, then packed individually or in whole bunches.

This festive dish is given a special lift by the addition of a caramelized sauce. Put the sugar, one tablespoon of water, and three drops of lemon juice into a pan, heat, then add a little liquid from cooking the chicken, which you will need to strain first. Bring it to the boil while blending with a whisk. Add a little salt and incorporate the cornstarch mixed to a smooth paste with a little water. Continue stirring over a gentle heat until the sauce is smooth and thick.

Using a sharp knife, bone the chicken, following the line of the breast bone to keep the rest of it whole. Reserve the giblets.

For the stuffing: Chop the scallions and brown in 4 tbsp olive oil. Stir in the rice, chopped garlic, white wine, and ½ cup/100 ml water. Cook for 10 minutes or until the liquid starts to reduce.

Next add the peeled, finely chopped chestnuts, pine nuts, raisins, and peeled and finely diced apple. Add chopped oregano, a little salt, stir and set aside.

Stuffed Chicken

Salt the chicken generously. Spoon the stuffing into the cavity until it is completely full.

Neatly sew the edges of the cavity together with kitchen string. Chop the carrot, celery, garlic, onion, potato, and leek. For the sauce: Heat the sugar in 1 tbsp water and the juice of ½ lemon. Set aside.

Put the giblets, vegetables, and chicken in a roasting pan. Add olive oil, salt, then cook in an oven at 465° F/240° C for 15 minutes. Add red wine, chopped tomatoes, and cook for 30 minutes. Blend the sauce with the strained cooking juices and thicken with cornstarch.

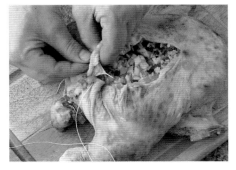

Chicken with

Preparation time:	*30 minutes*
Cooking time:	*20 minutes*
Difficulty:	*

Serves 4

1	chicken weighing 2¼ lb/1 kg
1 tbsp	olive oil
	salt
	pepper
1 tbsp	sweet mustard
3–4 tbsp	white wine
1 tsp	dried oregano
½ bunch	parsley
1	lemon
5½ oz/150 g	*graviera* cheese (Cretan Gruyère)
4	potatoes

To serve:

	arugula (rocket) leaves

Chicken with *graviera* is a very popular dish, especially in Crete. This nourishing dish, which is simple to make, can be enjoyed on any occasion.

These days chicken is eaten all over the world, but it was probably introduced to Greece by the Persians. Known as *kotopoulo* in Greek, chickens are raised in a free-range environment in villages across the hinterland. Choose chickens with plump lean flesh. A male bird can also be used in this recipe.

This judiciously flavored recipe uses the sort of simple produce so loved by Southern European cooks, and uses them in generous quantities. The indispensable olive oil adds warmth to the other ingredients as it releases its full fruity flavor.

According to mythology, there was a great battle between Athena, the goddess of war and wisdom, and Poseidon for the domination of Attica, which Athena won by making olive trees grow there, the symbol of peace. In the 1st century A.D. Dioscorides was already proclaiming the virtues of the olive tree in his writings: "The oil pressed from the green olive is perfect in the extreme and very good for the health."

The very image of Greek cuisine, chicken with *graviera* is a light dish. Oregano grows very well in this part of the world and is found in abundance around Ebaros in Crete. It is a close cousin of marjoram, but has a stronger taste.

Graviera meanwhile, is a firm textured cheese made from ewe's milk. It is a sort of Greek equivalent of Swiss Gruyère or Emmenthal, which you can use instead.

Use a sharp knife to cut off the white meat from the chicken into slices. Wash the arugula leaves and set aside.

Heat the olive oil in a skillet and brown the chicken, season. Put the mustard and white wine into a bowl, scatter on the oregano, and add to the chicken.

Cook over a low heat until all of the wine has evaporated.

Graviera

Add the chopped parsley and the lemon juice to the skillet with the chicken. Stir in the cubes of graviera.

Peel and grate the potatoes. Add some salt and leave to drain.

Cover the entire bottom of a nonstick skillet with the grated potato and dry cook. Turn the galette of potatoes onto the serving plate, spoon the chicken and the sauce into the middle and serve with arugula leaves.

Tzigerosarmas

Preparation time:	*40 minutes*
Cooking time:	*50 minutes*
Soaking time (lamb cauls):	*1 hour*
Difficulty:	★

Serves 4

2	lamb cauls
1½ lb/675 g	lamb offal (variety meats: liver, heart, kidneys, lungs, but not intestines)
	salt
4 tbsp	long grain rice
2 tbsp	olive oil

10	scallions
	pepper
2	lemons
1 bunch	dill
1 bunch	mint
3 cups/600 g	Greek, or thick, creamy yogurt
2	eggs

For the garnish:

	mint leaves
	paprika (optional)

Tzigerosarmas with Greek yogurt is an extremely popular dish in Greece, and originated in Thrace and Macedonia. Made from lamb offal, this traditional dish is usually eaten at Easter. It is easy to make and the name comes from the Turkish word for entrails, *tziger*, and the Greek word for rolled, *sarmas*, and it is a classic in this country's culinary repertoire.

In Ancient Greece, offal was never wasted. Long before the arrival of Christianity, pagan priests would sacrifice animals and present them as offerings to the gods.

In a world in which gods and goddesses ruled over the destiny of man, the oracles would examine the animal's entrails to try to decipher a divine message. After the ceremony, the holy men and their important guests would gather around the banqueting table. Homer described one such gathering in *The Odyssey*: "Entering into the hall of the divine Ulysses, they set down their cloaks on benches and chairs; then a fire would be lit under a large sheep and some fatted goats ... Having broiled the entrails, they shared them around."

In Greek cookery, many specialties give place of honor to red offal (the liver, heart, kidneys etc). Amongst the most popular are *splinantero*, stuffed intestine, or *cocoretsi*, which is made from beef. Our chef serves his *tzigerosarmas* with Greek yogurt.

Greeks eat a lot of cheese and dairy products, part of a diet derived from their rural, Mediterranean way of life. An indispensable ingredient, Greek yogurt, known locally as *yaourti* is particularly smooth and dense. It can be used sweetened or in savory dishes. Generally made from ewe's milk, it has an inimitable slightly sharp taste. You can use classic plain yogurt for this recipe, but drain it first.

Soak the lamb cauls for 1 hour in water. Drain. Wash the offal and bring to the boil in a large pan of salted water. Skim off any froth that forms then cook for about 10 minutes.

Leave the drained offal to cool then chop it into small pieces. Wash the rice.

Put 2 tbsp olive oil in a pan, fry the chopped scallions, then add the offal. Cook covered for 5 minutes. Add the rice, salt and pepper, sprinkle with lemon juice, and scatter with chopped dill and mint. Add 3–4 tbsp water, and cook for 10–15 minutes.

Line 4 ramekin dishes with pieces of caul and add the cooled filling. Trim the cauls.

Wrap each caul around the filling to form the shape of a large ball. Put them in a large dish, add a little water and cook in an oven preheated to 350° F/180° C for about 10 minutes.

Beat the yogurt with a whisk, add the eggs, and season. Whisk again, pour over the tzigerosarmas, and return to the oven for 10 minutes. Serve garnished with mint leaves and paprika.

Desserts & Pastries

Amygdalota

Preparation time	*20 minutes*
Cooking time:	*20 minutes*
Difficulty:	★

Serves 6

5 cups/480 g	ground almonds
4 cups/450 g	confectioners' sugar
1 tsp	vanilla extract
3	egg whites

½ cup/60 g	fine semolina
½ cup/100 g	candied cherries
2 tbsp	orange flower water

Many of the islands in the Aegean Sea have their own recipes for the mouth-watering little cakes with almonds, or *amygdalota* in Greek. The recipes all differ slightly according to whether you're on Andros, Hydra, Skyros, Skopelos, Mykonos, Patmos, or even Siphnos. In olden days, the islanders on Andros used to give *amygdalota* to people who were getting married, the symbolism of the almond tree having both mythological links (the promise of virility and fecundity) and Christian links because the casing around the kernel was likened to the Virgin protecting the infant Jesus. These days, Greeks like nothing better than to nibble on them as they sip the local, strong, black, and very sweet coffee.

All recipes for *amygdalota* have one thing in common – they use almonds, or roughly crushed almonds known as *amygdale*. The almond tree is a member of the rose family and its magnificent white flowers blossom very early in the year, followed by the leaves, and finally the fruit, which is picked between the end of August and the beginning of September. Encased in a downy, soft pale green husk, they are shelled and dried before they are sold.

Some recipes use crumbled cookies or breadcrumbs instead of the semolina to make the dough. Others suggest the addition of grated lemon, orange, or mandarin rind.

To give your *amygdalota* a pretty shape, our chef suggests you use an ice-cream scoop to mold them into little domes. You could also shape them into little "sausages" or use a pastry bag to pipe them into spirals on nonstick baking parchment. That way, they won't burn on the bottom.

When you take them out of the oven, sprinkle the *amygdalota* with a few drops of orange flower water or rose water. They'll disappear before your eyes!

Put the almonds into a bowl. Add 2½ cups/270 g confectioners' sugar and the vanilla extract.

Whisk 3 egg whites into a soft foam and fold them into the almonds and sugar.

Add the semolina. Stir briskly until it forms into a dough.

Line a baking pan with nonstick baking parchment. Use an ice-cream scoop to shape small domes of dough and arrange them on the baking sheet.

Decorate each one with half a candied cherry. Cook in an oven preheated to 340° F/170° C for about 20 minutes.

Sprinkle the cakes with the orange flower water as soon as you take them out of the oven. Sift the remaining confectioners' sugar over the top. Serve cold.

Bougatsa

Preparation time:	*25 minutes*
Cooking time:	*20 minutes*
Difficulty:	✶

Serves 4

6	cardamom seeds
1¾ cups/400 ml	milk
4 tbsp/50 g	sugar
½ cup/85 g	coarse semolina
1	egg

2 tbsp	butter
8 sheets	phyllo (filo) pastry

For the garnish:

	confectioners' sugar
	ground cinnamon

In Ancient Greece the cooking skills of a young girl of marriageable age were judged by the people of her village. The future bride would have to demonstrate her abilities in particular by making *bougatsa*, a traditional cake made with tissue-thin sheets of phyllo (filo) pastry and milk, a combination loved by Greeks everywhere. This is still a popular dish with families and can be enjoyed on any occasion.

These days Greeks often eat *bougatsa* for breakfast. It's full of calories for energy and is also known as *galactopita*.

It has a very rich filling made from milk, sugar, egg, and butter flavored with cardamom. This aromatic herb originated from the Malabar coast of India. The cardamom seeds are encased in a bean and when dried are used as an oriental spice. Slightly piquant, cardamom adds a wonderful perfume to rice and sweet pastries. Our chef says you could use orange, mandarin, or even lemon instead.

Nothing can take the place of the phyllo. Typically Greek, these tissue-thin sheets of pastry are normally circular in shape and were originally made by the *karagounides*, herdsmen, of rural Thessalia. If left uncovered, the phyllo tends to dry out very quickly and starts to crumble, so leave the pile of sheets wrapped in a damp cloth. You can also buy it ready made from supermarkets and from specialist delicatessens.

According to Greek tradition, the *bougatsa* is often served at the table cut into small squares. In some families it is served with a small glass of wine.

Grind the tiny black cardamom seeds with a mortar and pestle and scrape them into a pan. Heat for 1 minute then add the milk and sugar, whisking continuously.

When it reaches boiling point, add the sifted semolina. Continue stirring until it forms into a smooth creamy texture.

Remove from the heat, wait until it is lukewarm then whisk in the egg and 1 tbsp butter. Melt the remaining butter and set aside.

Lay one sheet of phyllo pastry on one half of a baking pan, then use another sheet to line the other half. Use the remaining sheets of pastry to completely line the dish, making sure you leave a good overhang all the way around. Use a pastry brush to baste it with some melted butter.

Tip the cardamom-flavored cream filling into the phyllo-lined pan.

Bring up the folds of the overhanging pastry and lay them on top of each other so that the filling is totally encased. Baste the top with the remaining butter. Bake in an oven at 400° F/200° C for 10–15 minutes. Turn out, and cut into squares. Dust with confectioners' sugar and cinnamon.

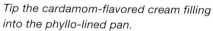

Brioche Flavored with

Preparation time: 1 hour
Cooking time: 45 minutes
Resting/rising time (dough): 2 hours
                          15 minutes
Difficulty: ★★

Serves 4

2½ oz/70 g	fresh yeast (or 5 tsp dried)
1¾ cups/400 ml	milk
3 lb 5 oz/1.5 kg	white bread flour
1¾ cups/400 g	sugar

6	eggs
1 tsp	ground mastic
9 oz/250 g	butter
½ cup/50 g	slivered almonds

In Greek families that observe the Orthodox religion, Easter symbolizes both joy and abundance. After the long weeks of simple Lenten fare, during which the consumption of certain foodstuffs is prohibited, cooks can again concoct delicious recipes with unrivaled flavors.

On the beautiful island of Chios, the locals make a delicious brioche flavored with mastic. Decorated with eggs that are painted red, a symbol of the blood of Christ and of the Life Eternal, this traditional specialty is eaten everywhere. When it comes out of the oven, the guests carefully examine the surface of the brioche for cracks, which are rumored to be harbingers of luck and happiness in the home!

This specialty can be enjoyed at any time of the year. Our chef recommends that you cover the dough, which is made from yeast, flour, sugar, and milk, with a cloth before it is left to rise. Do not open the oven door while it is cooking!

This delicately perfumed brioche gives off the characteristic aroma of mastic. Extracted from the trunk and branches of the lentisc or mastic tree, a bush that has grown for thousands of years on the island of Chios, the resin is extracted by making incisions with a sharp tool. Mastic is widely used in Greek, Turkish, and Moroccan cookery and can be found in resin or crystal form in specialty stores. It is usually pounded in a pestle and mortar.

Lentisc trees also grow in the eastern Mediterranean, South America, and North Africa. The ones from the island of Chios are said to ooze mastic "tears." The locals will tell you that this phenomenon dates back to the very beginnings of Christianity. When St Isidore begged them to do so, the bushes would start to weep!

Designed to be shared, *Paska* brioche is traditionally broken into pieces by hand and generously shared with guests.

Put the yeast and 1 cup/250 ml warm milk into a bowl (if using dried yeast, follow maker's instructions). Mix with the fingers. Add 2 cups/250 g flour and ¾ cup/200 g sugar. Mix and knead. Leave to rest for 30 minutes.

Put 5 eggs and the remaining sugar into a food processor and blend until the mixture is very pale.

Add the egg and sugar mix to the yeast preparation. Mix again with the fingers. Mix in the remaining flour, remaining warm milk, ground mastic, and melted butter. After a final mix leave to rise for 1 hour.

Ground Mastic

Sprinkle some flour onto the work surface. Shape the dough into balls, then roll out into long rope shapes.

Overlap three ropes of dough then plait them. Put them on a sheet of nonstick paper and leave to rest for 45 minutes.

Beat the remaining egg and use it to glaze the brioche. Sprinkle on the slivered almonds and bake in an oven preheated to 350° F/180° C for about 45 minutes.

Christopsomo

½ cup/100 g	sugar		1 tsp	ground cinnamon
1 oz/30 g	fresh yeast		1 tsp	ground cardamom
	(or 2 tsp dried)		1 tsp	ground anise
1 lb 10 oz/750 g	white bread flour		3½ tbsp	white wine
1	orange		1½ tsp	salt
			scant ½ cup/	
			100 ml	olive oil
			1½ cups/150 g	walnut pieces
			1 cup/100 g	white raisins
			1 tbsp	sesame seeds
			1 tbsp	nigella seeds
			4	whole walnuts in their shells

Preparation time: 30 minutes
Cooking time: 1 hour
Resting time (yeast dough): 30 minutes
Rising time (bread): about 1 hour
Difficulty: ★★

Serves 4

True masters of the art of cake making, Greeks have recipes for every occasion: Christmas (*christopsomo*), Easter (*lazari, lambrokouloures*), St Fanourios's Day (*fanouropites*), St Dimitri's Day (*dimitrikouloures*), to say nothing of christenings, engagements, and marriages.

Christopsomo, "bread of Christ" in Greek is eaten on Christmas Eve. The virgin olive oil, raisins, and other dried fruit mark it out from ordinary breads. Making it is a ritual: lighting the fire, mixing and kneading the dough, shaping it, decorating it, and so on. It is always decorated with a large X, the first letter of the word "Christ" in Greek. Before it is cut, the head of the family crosses himself/herself, wishes everybody a happy Christmas and then breaks the bread and shares it around. In Lefkas, the island home of our chef, a lucky charm is inserted into the dough before cooking. The bread is broken in half and wine is poured onto it three times in memory of the blood of Christ.

The water used to prepare the yeast dough must be warm. If it is too cool, or, conversely, too hot or boiling, it will kill the action of the yeast. The rising time depends on the quality of the yeast, the ambient temperature, and the temperature of the water.

After thoroughly mixing the dough, knead it firmly with both thumbs. You should end up with a fairly soft consistency. The top is decorated in the shape of a cross and often a seal engraved with religious symbols. In some villages, the older women sculpt the bread into the shape of flowers, birds, and agricultural instruments.

Sesame and nigella seeds are sprinkled over the top. According to local belief, sesame seeds symbolize life and fecundity. Nigella, meanwhile, keeps werewolves and demons away, which emerge from the earth just before Christmas to spoil human happiness.

For the dough: Mix 1 pinch sugar, the crumbled yeast, 3 tbsp flour and a dash of warm water in a bowl. If using dried yeast, follow maker's instructions. Leave for 30 minutes until the yeast starts to foam.

Put the remaining flour in a large bowl. Add the yeast mixture, grated orange peel, remaining sugar, cinnamon, cardamom and anise, wine, and salt. Knead well and add a little warm water and 5 tbsp olive oil.

When the dough is smooth and elastic, add the walnut pieces and the raisins. Knead again and shape the dough into a ball (reserving a piece the size of an orange).

Grease an 8-in/28-cm cake pan and sprinkle it with some sesame seeds. Put the dough in the pan and press it flat. Roll out 2 long rope shapes from the reserved dough and arrange them on top of the other dough in the shape of a cross.

Dampen your hands and smooth the surface of the bread. Scatter on the nigella and remaining sesame seeds.

After trimming the 4 ends of the "cross," press in the whole walnuts, still in their shells. Cover with a double cloth and leave to rise for 45–60 minutes or until the dough has doubled in volume. Bake in an oven preheated to 350° F/175° C for 1 hour.

Preparation time:	*30 minutes*
Cooking time:	*35 minutes*
Soaking time (tomatoes):	*12 hours*
Soaking time (carrots):	*2 hours*
Difficulty:	★

Serves 4

10	baby Santorini or cherry tomatoes
10	baby carrots
2 tbsp	lime juice
4 tbsp	sugar

1	vanilla bean
1 stick	cinnamon
	zest from ½ orange
1 tsp	ground alum
½	lemon
3–4 tbsp	thyme honey

For the garnish:

¼ cup/30 g	almonds
2 sprigs	mint

A symbol of hospitality, Greek sweetmeats are traditionally served to afternoon visitors. Made in generous quantities by every family, these pieces of tender vegetables or fruit are cooked in syrup then arranged in a large dish. Everybody has their own spoon and helps themselves from the platter, which is usually accompanied by a glass of water.

These elegant little sweetmeats, known as *glyca tou koutaliou* in Greece, were a favorite as far back as the Byzantine Age. In the 1920s, Greeks born in Asia Minor helped to spread the word about these specialties, particularly in the Cyclades. The original recipe has been handed down from generation to generation ever since.

They come in an infinite variety of forms as they are usually made with regional produce. On the island of Chios, for instance, bergamot is used, in Andros lemon blossom, in Serifos cherries, in Larissa watermelon, and in Aigion baby eggplant. Sotiris Evangelou has chosen small tomatoes and baby carrots for his version.

Easy to make, these sweetmeats are full of Eastern flavors. After blanching the vegetables or fruit, they need to be soaked for a few hours in the lime juice or, if preferred, in lemon. This vital part of the operation helps them to keep their shape. And don't forget to wash them well before you cook them in the sugar syrup.

Cleverly flavored with cinnamon, vanilla, and orange zest, the syrup needs to be sufficiently thick. To achieve this our chef adds some ground alum, specific to the Essaouira region of Morocco's Atlantic coast. But you can get the same result by replacing it with the juice of a lemon.

In Greece, these little sweetmeats are stored in glass preserve jars where they will keep for several months.

Make a cross-shaped slit in the skins of the tomatoes, cover with boiling water for about 1 minute, refresh in ice water, and peel. Discard the leaves from the carrots, blanch for 3 minutes in boiling water, and refresh.

Fill a small bowl with water and 1 tbsp lime juice. Add the tomatoes and leave to soak for 12 hours. In another small bowl filled with water and the remaining lime juice leave the carrots to soak for 2 hours. Rinse thoroughly.

For the syrup: Heat a pan of water with the sugar, vanilla bean, cinnamon stick, and orange zest and cook for about 15 minutes.

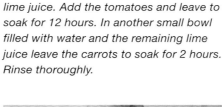

Sweetmeats

Sprinkle the alum onto the syrup. Add slices of lemon and the carrots and cook for about 3 minutes.

Now add the tomatoes and cook for 12 minutes. Remove the carrots and tomatoes from the syrup.

Take the pan off the heat and pour the honey into the syrup. Add the tomatoes and carrots. Serve the Greek sweetmeats on a platter decorated with almonds, mint, and the vanilla pod.

Fanouropita

Preparation time: 20 minutes
Cooking time: 30-40 minutes

Difficulty: ★

Serves 4

2 cups/500 ml	fresh orange juice
1 cup/250 ml	virgin olive oil
1½ cups/350 g	superfine sugar
½ cup/125 g	black treacle (or molasses)
4⅓ cups/500 g	all-purpose flour
1 tsp	bicarbonate of soda
½ tbsp	ground cloves
½ tbsp	ground cinnamon
	nutmeg
1½ cups/175 g	raisins
¾ cup/85 g	crushed walnuts

Many Greeks call upon St Fanourios to help them find missing people or animals, even things they have lost. His saint's day is celebrated on August 27. Any woman seeking his help will bake one of these cakes and take it to the church for it to be blessed. There is therefore real competition between cooks as to who produces the best and most appetizing *fanouropita*. After Mass, the cakes are shared out and enjoyed either at the church, or exchanged between neighbors and eaten later with the family.

Fanouropita is a soft textured sort of Greek gingerbread, characterized by the lingering taste of cinnamon and nutmeg, the crunchy nuts, soft raisins and an after-taste of caramel. It uses neither eggs nor milk, which means it can be eaten during the fasting periods dictated by the Orthodox Church.

Our cake is enriched with black treacle and raisins. However, if you prefer, instead of the treacle, use a good, well-flavored Greek honey.

Raisins have been exported from the port of Patras in the Peloponnese since the 14th century. Three varieties of grape in particular are dried: sultana, very sweet small white grapes; Corinthian, small black ones; Muscat raisins from Alexandria, which are also white. After harvesting, they are left to dry in the sun for 8–12 days.

Don't be surprised if the top of this *fanouropita* quickly turns a dark brown in the heat of the oven. This is due to the presence of olive oil, nuts, black treacle, cinnamon, and ground cloves. You can remedy this by covering the pan with baking foil towards the end of the cooking time.

Put the orange juice, olive oil, and sugar into a bowl and whisk rapidly.

Add the black treacle and stir again.

Next add the sifted flour and bicarbonate of soda. Keep whisking until all of the flour has been incorporated.

Sprinkle on the ground cloves, cinnamon, a few scapings of nutmeg, and continue whisking.

Finally add the raisins and the roughly crushed walnuts to the cake batter. Whisk for one last time.

Tip the mixture into a round non-stick cake pan. Cook in an oven preheated to 340° F/170° C for 30–40 minutes. Turn out and serve cold.

Mastic Ice Cream on a Nest of

Preparation time: 25 minutes
Cooking time: 25 minutes
Difficulty: ☆

Serves 4

scant ¾ cup/150 g sugar
10 oz/300 g morello cherries, pitted
7 oz/200 g *kadaifi* (Greek angelhair noodles)

For the mastic ice cream:
1 cup/250 ml whole milk
1 cup/250 ml heavy cream
generous ½ cup/ 125 g sugar
5 egg yolks
½ tsp ground mastic (see below)

For the garnish:
mint leaves

This succulent, easy to make Greek dessert is a wonderful marriage of textures and flavors. This much-loved dish is famous for its sweetness offset by the characteristic taste of the mastic and the crunchiness of the *kadaifi*.

Kadaifi are made from flour, salt, and water and come in long strands of "angel hair." To give them their characteristic shape the dough is put through a round metal disk perforated with tiny holes. Also available in good delicatessens, these "angel hair" noodles are used in the making of a variety of cakes and pastries. In this recipe the *kadaifi* must first be plaited before being shaped into a round loop and the ends loosely tied. Our chef then uses a pair of scissors to trim the ends and pops the trimmings in the middle of the nest.

Greeks have a very sweet tooth and often eat cake served with mastic ice cream. Mastic comes from the long-living mastic or lentisc tree that flourishes on the island of Chios. Its small beads of yellow resin are always used very sparingly. Widely found in both Greek and Turkish cookery, mastic is the ancestor of chewing-gum. At the time of the Ottoman empire the ladies of the sultan's harem would chew it to sweeten their breath! Usually found in resin or crystal form in Greek, Middle Eastern, or North African specialty stores, it has to be ground in a pestle and mortar or wrapped in paper and smashed with a hammer.

This elegant dessert is enhanced with morello cherries in syrup. Originally from Asia Minor, these little cherries with their slightly sour taste were already a favorite with Ancient Greeks. The traditional way of preparing them is to stone them before dipping them in water with some sugar. The syrup is then sharpened with the juice of a lemon. Some cooks occasionally add some *moshos* leaves, a Greek aromatic plant.

For the ice cream: Bring the milk, heavy cream, and half of the sugar just up to boiling point in a heavy-bottomed pan.

In a bowl, beat the egg yolks with the remaining sugar and slowly add the hot cream beating continously. Return to the pan and stir over low heat until it thickens, add the ground mastic. Churn the cooled mixture in an ice-cream maker.

Make a syrup by heating a scant ¾ cup/ 150 g sugar in ⅔ cup/150 ml water. Add the cherries.

Kadaifi and Morello Cherries

Spread out the kadaifi and separate the strands into 12 portions. Smooth them into 12 long ribbons, twist each ribbon loosely, and trim the ends.

Lay out 3 ribbons of kadaifi and plait them tightly. Make another 3 plaits.

Shape the plait into a round "nest" and bake in an oven preheated to 320° F/ 160° C for 10–15 minutes. Arrange each nest on a plate, put a scoop of ice cream in the center, surround with cherries, and coat with syrup. Garnish with mint.

Kadaifi

Preparation time:	40 minutes
Cooking time:	30 minutes
Cooling time (base):	1 hour
Cooling time (finished kadaifi):	2 hours
Difficulty:	★★

Serves 6–8

For the kadaifi base:

1 lb 2 oz/500 g	kadaifi (Greek angelhair noodles)
1½ cups/150 g	coarsely chopped pistachios
4 tbsp	melted butter

For the syrup :

2 cups/450	sugar

1	cinnamon stick
1	lemon

For the confectioners' custard:

2 cups/500 ml	milk
6 tbsp	superfine sugar
1	lemon
2 tbsp	all-purpose flour
1 tbsp	cornstarch
1 tsp	vanilla extract
2	eggs
	salt
1 tbsp	butter

For the Chantilly cream:

2 cups/500 g	heavy cream
2 tbsp	confectioners' sugar
1 tsp	vanilla extract

The windows of pastry shops in Greek villages are full of tempting treats: little cakes shaped like crescent moons, stars or cones generously sprinkled with almonds, pistachios, sesame seeds, or chocolate, *kadaifi* smothered in cream, *baklavas* dripping with syrup. The shops do a roaring trade all day long.

Chrysanthi Stamkopoulos brings you this original recipe for *kadaifi* that she has named for the village where she was born, Neraida in western Macedonia. This mouth-watering dish takes *kadaifi* noodles and dresses them up with oven-roasted chopped pistachios coated with syrup then topped with confectioners' custard and Chantilly cream.

Kadaifi noodles are produced commercially. They are long, white, very fine strands that might be likened to "angel hair." Carefully tease the strands apart so you can hide the coarsely chopped pistachios in the middle of the *kadaifi*

nest. Everything is then coated with melted butter and sprinkled with water. To do this, put the dish near the sink, put your fingers under a very gently running tap and spray the mixture with drops of water by flicking your fingers. Gently moistened like this, the *kadaifi* will cook more uniformly, will not split when it is turned out and will be nice and crunchy. As soon as it has browned, take it out of the oven and immediately douse it in the hot syrup.

Pistachio nuts, *keliphoto* in Greek, are grown in many regions, primarily Aegina, an island in the Gulf of Salonika, but also Makri in central Greece and Markopolou in Attica.

The *kadaifi* will be topped with confectioners' custard and Chantilly cream. Just smooth on a flat layer, make a pattern with a spatula or even pipe on some little peaks with a pastry bag. Refrigerate for at least two hours so that the flavor of the cream impregnates the mix and softens it.

Put the kadaifi into an ovenproof dish, sprinkle with 1 cup/100 g pistachios and mix. Pour on the melted butter and using your fingers sprinkle with some water. Bake in an oven at 320° F/160° C until the base is golden brown.

For the syrup: In a pan bring to the boil 3 cups/750 ml water, the sugar, cinnamon, and some slices of lemon. Remove from the heat. As soon as the kadaifi comes out of the oven, drizzle over the hot syrup. Cool for 1 hour at room temperature.

For the confectioners' custard: Put the milk, sugar, and finely grated lemon peel into a heavy-bottomed pan and bring slowly to boiling point.

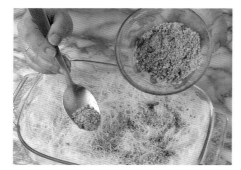

Neraida

In a bowl whisk the flour, cornstarch, vanilla extract, eggs, and a pinch of salt to a smooth paste with a dash of milk. Slowly add the hot milk, beating continuously. Transfer to a pan and whisk over low heat until it thickens. Stir in the butter and leave to cool.

Using a plastic scraper, transfer the confectioners' custard onto the kadaifi base and smooth it flat. Chill to set.

Top with chantilly cream, made by beating the cream to soft peaks and adding the sugar, and vanilla extract. Use a palette knife to smooth this over the custard then scatter with the remaining pistachios. Chill for 2 hours. Cut into small squares.

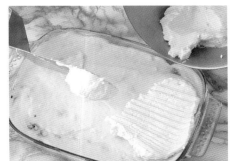

Karidopita

Preparation time:	30 minutes
Cooking time:	50 minutes
Difficulty:	★

Serves 6

For the cake mix:

5 oz/150 g	butter
¾ cup/175 g	superfine sugar
5	eggs
2½ cups/300 g	flour
1 tsp	dried yeast
1 cup/85 g	walnut kernels

1	orange
1 cup/250 ml	milk

For the syrup:

½	lemon
1	clove
1 stick	cinnamon
1½ cups/325 g	superfine sugar

For the garnish:

2 tbsp	morello cherries
	orange segments

Karidopita is a cake made with nuts sprinkled with a flavored syrup. It is always a winner whether served for lunch or enjoyed with a cup of coffee. It's been a specialty among pastry chefs from Ioaninna in Epirus for the last 100 years.

Depending on the inventiveness of the cook, the ingredients in the *karidopita* may vary. Some cooks flavor the mixture with alcohol or with spices (cinnamon, cloves). Others replace the flour with a mixture of dried breadcrumbs and chopped almonds, or with fine semolina.

This recipe is fairly simple to make. Before you start, leave the butter to come up to room temperature because it will be easier when you come to mix the ingredients. And always beat the butter and sugar before adding the eggs, flour, and dried yeast. Your cake will also be lighter if you separate the eggs, whisk the whites in a separate bowl and fold them in at the last moment.

Walnuts and orange make a wonderful combination. The nuts from Pelion in Thessalia, with their tasty white flesh, are a real favorite with Greeks. Oranges were known as long ago as Ancient Greece. According to mythology, Heracles brought back these "golden apples" from the garden of the Hesperides to Mycenae as one of his Twelve Labors. Lemons originated from China and the Himalayas. Arab merchants had introduced them all around the Mediterranean basin by the 12th century.

To test whether the *karidopita* is cooked, insert the tip of a sharp knife. When it comes out clean the cake is done.

Karidopita is traditionally baked in a large rectangular pan and decorated with lozenge shapes, but you can do what our chef has done here and use a round pan instead (the chef has filled a pastry case as a variation). Decorate the cake with orange segments and morello cherries.

Put the softened butter, cut into cubes, into a bowl and add the superfine sugar. Beat together.

Add the eggs, one by one.

Add the sifted flour mixed with the dried yeast. Stir rapidly with a spoon then pour everything into a food processor and blend until it forms into a light "dough."

Return the batter to the bowl and add the roughly chopped walnuts and grated orange rind.

Lastly mix in the milk. Pour the batter into a greased baking tin and bake in an oven preheated to 350° F/180° C for 50 minutes. Turn out onto a shallow dish.

For the syrup: Bring ½ cup/125 ml water to the boil with the lemon, clove, cinnamon, and sugar. Remove from the heat to cool a little, then pour over the karidopita. Serve decorated with morello cherries and orange segments.

Kourambiedes

Preparation time:	40 minutes
Cooking time:	15 minutes
Difficulty:	★

Serves 10

14 oz/400 g	butter
6 oz/175 g	butter made with olive oil
1 cup/225 g	confectioners' sugar
2 lb 6 oz/1.2 kg	all-purpose flour
1 tsp	baking powder

½ tsp	bicarbonate of soda
1	vanilla bean
3–4 tbsp	brandy
1¾ cups/250 g	chopped almonds
¾ cup/85 g	whole almonds
3–4 tbsp	rose water

For the garnish:

confectioners' sugar

Kourambiedes are delicious little cakes made with almonds. Dredged in confectioners' sugar and perfumed with rose water, they are popular all over Greece, especially at Christmas time.

Easy to make, the starring role goes to the almonds. A firm favorite since Ancient Greece, almonds originated in Asia Minor. The Romans used to call them "Greek nuts." Grown now primarily in Larissa in Thessalia, they are picked from August to September. Laid out on tarpaulins or nets, they are shelled then left to dry. If you want to skin almond kernels, put them into water which is just at boiling point for one minute then let them cool. When rubbed between thumb and finger, the skin will slip off.

In mythology, the almond tree was associated with the story of Phyllis, daughter of the King of Thrace and her betrothed, Demonphon, the son of Theseus. Demonphon was sent off to war and promised the young girl that he would soon return. But receiving no news from him and feeling abandoned, Phyllis killed herself and was turned into an almond tree. Learning of the catastrophic mistake, Demonphon threw his arms around the tree, which burst into leaf and blossom.

These extremely elegant little cakes exude the flavors of the East thanks to the rose water. Used particularly for making Turkish Delight, this decoction subtly perfumes many sweetmeats. In some regions of Greece lemon flower water is used instead, or even orange flower water, known as *anthonero* in Greek.

Kourambiedes are traditionally served in generous quantities to guests, accompanied by a glass of water.

Melt the butters and whisk them in a bowl with the confectioners' sugar.

In another bowl, sift the flour, baking powder, bicarbonate of soda, and all the seeds scraped from the vanilla bean. Add to the butter and sugar and mix until it forms a smooth dough. Add the brandy.

Add the chopped almonds and blend with your fingers.

Turn out the dough onto a floured work board and roll out to a rectangle. Use a cookie cutter to cut into rounds.

Make a depression in the middle of each with your thumb and press in one almond. Place on a nonstick baking sheet and bake in an oven preheated to 400° F/200° C for 15 minutes.

Use a pastry brush to baste the kourambiedes with rose water. Dredge with confectioners' sugar and arrange on a plate.

Loukoumades

Preparation time: 35 minutes
Cooking time: 15 minutes
Resting time (dough):   2 hours
Difficulty: ☆

Serves 4

3 oz/85 g	fresh yeast (or 6 tsp dried)
3 tbsp	olive oil
1¾ cups/400 ml	milk
6 tbsp	sugar

4⅓ cups/500 g	all-purpose flour
	salt
1	egg white
4 cups/1 l	frying oil
1½ tbsp	pine honey
1 tbsp	sesame seeds
1 tsp	ground cinnamon (optional)

Loukoumades are delicious little doughnuts smothered in honey and they are extremely popular in Greece. Usually made for religious festivals, they are served to guests in generous quantities and are particularly good hot.

Particularly prized in Crete and the Cyclades, *loukoumades* are bursting with Eastern flavors. Similar recipes are also found in Asia Minor. The word *loukoum* comes from the Turkish for "delicacy," a reminder of their geographical origin. These little doughnuts have been around for centuries and even found their way into the 11th-century *Tales of A Thousand and One Nights*.

Small and round, it is vital that the *loukoumades* are made fresh and fried in boiling hot oil. The rope of dough is squeezed between the thumb and index finger and scooped into little balls using a spoon. When you take them out of the oil you might want to drain them on paper towels.

This recipe uses honey to coat the doughnuts. This sweet, delicate product is made from nectar from flowers collected by bees, and is a great source of energy. According to Greek mythology, the baby Zeus was hidden by his mother in Crete and fed on honey. Our chef suggests you look for pine honey, famous in Greece for its outstanding aroma.

These elegant little doughnuts are finished with sesame seeds. These are used for lots of sweet pastries in Greece, and are also the key ingredient in the famous *halva*, which also includes honey and almonds.

In some areas of Greece the *loukoumades* are lightly sprinkled with ground cinnamon, an indispensable spice in Eastern cookery.

Put the fresh yeast into a bowl, add 3 tsp olive oil. If using dried yeast, follow maker's instructions. Warm the milk in a pan.

Pour the warm milk onto the yeast and whisk.

Sift the sugar and flour together into a separate bowl and add a pinch of salt. Add to the the yeast mixture.

Beat the yeast and flour mixture with a whisk until it turns into a slightly soft dough. Leave to rest for 2 hours.

Whisk the egg white until stiff. Add this to the dough and fold in.

Squeeze the dough between the fingers and thumb and use a spoon to shape into balls. Fry in small batches in hot oil until they float to the surface. Drain on paper towels. Place in a shallow dish, pour over the honey, and scatter with toasted sesame seeds and cinnamon. Serve hot.

Mbourekakia

Preparation time:	40 minutes
Cooking time:	30 minutes
Refrigeration time (filling):	2 hours
Resting time (dough):	15 minutes
Difficulty	✭

Serves 4

4 cups\1 l	corn oil for frying

For the dough:

2 cups/250 g	all-purpose flour
4 tbsp	olive oil

For the filling:

½ cup/100 g	pudding rice
1¼ cups/300 ml	milk
4 tbsp	sugar
1	vanilla bean
½ tsp	cornstarch

For the garnish:

	confectioners' sugar
	ground cinnamon

Mbourekakia are delicious little "pasties" from the island of Chios and depending on the filling they can be sweet, as in our recipe, or savory. They are popular during the carnival period when every village organizes a huge banquet and they are given to children in fancy dress costumes.

Easy to make, *mbourekakia* can be enjoyed on any occasion. The rice is the uncontested star of the filling. Now eaten the world over, this cereal was being produced in China thousands of years ago. It was imported into Turkistan and Mesopotamia by the Persians. Alexander the Great later introduced it to the Ancient Greeks, having brought it back with him from his expedition to India.

In this recipe the rice is cooked in milk and it must be left to rest for two hours. The delicious filling gives off the unmistakable aroma of vanilla. Vanilla beans, the only edible fruit of the orchid family, were introduced to Spain by the Conquistadors in the 16th century. Legend has it that Spanish soldiers discovered vanilla for the first time when tasting Aztec cocoa beans. Seduced by the unusual taste of the vanilla, Iberians gave it the name *vaynillia*, which means "little seeds." The fame of these beans quickly exceeded the frontiers of the Peninsula and spread all over Europe.

For that finishing touch, the *mbourekakia* are lightly dusted with ground cinnamon. This spice is also very widely used in Moroccan cookery, and is available either ground or in sticks. Appreciated for its penetrating aroma, its warm and piquant flavor adds a lift to many sweet and savory dishes.

These little carnival "pasties" are always a great favorite with children.

For the filling: Put the rice into a pan with 1¼ cups/300 ml water. Cook for 15 minutes or until the water has been absorbed.

Add the milk to the pan and stir with a wooden spatula. Add sugar to taste.

Split the vanilla bean lengthwise and add to the pan. Add the cornstarch, mixed to a paste with a little water, and cook until thick. Refrigerate for 2 hours, then remove the vanilla bean.

Sift the flour into a bowl, add the olive oil and mix by hand, gradually adding sufficient cold water to make a pastry dough. Leave to rest for 15 minutes.

Roll out the pastry thinly into a rectangle on a floured surface. Add 1 tsp of the filling at regular intervals.

Fold the pastry once over the filling along its longest edge, then fold over on itself once more. Cut along the second folded edge, then cut the flattened roll into sections. Repeat until the pastry is finished. Fry in very hot corn oil. Drain, and serve dusted with the sugar and cinnamon.

Apples Stuffed with

Preparation time: 30 minutes
Cooking time: 45 minutes
Difficulty: ★

Serves 6

6	large red apples
1 cup/100 g	walnut kernels
1¼ cups/250 g	superfine sugar
2 tsp	ground cinnamon
½ cup/55 g	raisins

scant ½ cup/ 120 ml	Metaxa brandy
3 tbsp	butter
4 tbsp	extra-virgin olive oil

Simple to make and delicious to eat, apples stuffed with dried fruit are popular throughout Greece. In summer Greeks eat this dessert warm with vanilla ice cream or *kaymak*, a thick cream specific to Greek and Turkish cookery.

Miltos Karoubas recommends that you choose red dessert apples for this recipe. In Greece the great majority of apples come from mountainous areas with a cool climate, such as western Macedonia (Florina, Kastoria, and Rodochori). The poet Homer was already praising the virtues of apples. When the nymph Thetis married the mortal Peleus, Eris, goddess of discord, tossed a golden apple bearing the inscription "to the most beautiful one." Athena, goddess of wisdom, the sciences and arts, quarreled with Hera (goddess of love) over the fruit. Zeus refused to nominate "the most beautiful one," so Paris, son of the King of Troy was asked to decide. Seduced by her beauty, he gave the fruit to Aphrodite.

In a new departure, our chef suggests you core the apples from the bottom using a small curved knife or an apple corer, but not all the way through. This gives the apple a wider base to sit on and the filling stays inside rather than spilling out onto the cooking pan.

This filling is made from chopped walnuts (or you can use a mixture of walnuts and almonds if you prefer). The raisins won't need to be soaked in advance as the Metaxa brandy added to the filling allows them to swell inside the apples. Ordinary three-star Metaxa is used for cooking, but older types can have up to seven stars and are for sipping!

Each guest is served with a stuffed apple lightly sprinkled with cinnamon.

Wash and dry the apples. Using an apple corer remove the core and seeds, working from the base, but do not bore right through.

For the stuffing: Mix the chopped nuts, ¾ cup/200 g of the sugar, the cinnamon and raisins in a bowl.

Add the Metaxa and stir well.

Dried Fruit

Use a small teaspoon to fill the cavity of each apple with the nut stuffing.

Arrange the apples, open end upward, in an ovenproof dish.

Melt the butter and oil in a pan and spoon over the apples. Scatter over some sugar. Bake in an oven at 350° F/180° C for about 45 minutes. Serve warm, surrounded by the cooking liquid and sprinkled with cinnamon.

Sperna

Preparation time:	20 minutes
Cooking time:	10 minutes
Drying time (wheat):	6–8 hours
Difficulty:	★

Serves 4

1½ cups/250 g	durum wheat
	salt
¾ cup/100 g	chopped almonds
¾ cup/85 g	walnut pieces
¾ cup/100g	sesame seeds
1¾ cups/200 g	black raisins
1 cup/100 g	white raisins

½ cup/100 g	multicolored dragees
1	pomegranate
1 scant tsp	ground cinnamon
1 tsp	grated cardamom
1 tsp	ground coriander
1 tsp	ground cumin
1 tbsp	fine breadcrumbs

To serve:

	superfine sugar or honey

In some parts of Greece, when a family wants to celebrate a member's saint's day they use a recipe for cooked wheat, dried fruits, and spices known as *sperna*. This dish is blessed in the church and then shared by the guest of honor and the family. Arranged in a big shallow dish, it is decorated with brightly colored dragees. The guests help themselves then add sugar to taste. Throughout Greece *sperna* is also made to symbolize the eternal rest of the deceased, when it is called *kolyva*. On certain days, Greeks honor the memory of the dead by making an offering of *kolyva*. Shaped into a dome, it is covered with dried breadcrumbs and confectioners' sugar – tiny, silver-ball cake decorations are used to pick out the name of the deceased.

All of these customs date back to Ancient Greece, when a similar recipe was known as *panspermia*, an offering to the gods (in particular Demeter, goddess of the harvest) and to the Greeks' ancestors.

The durum wheat that forms the basic ingredient of the *sperna* is still sacred to the Greeks, being the symbol of the earth and the basis of all foods. When cooking wheat, nobody ever pours away the juice. Instead it is reduced down a little before dried apricots, grapes, spices etc. are added and then mashed. Others mix it with honey and drink it. In our recipe, sugar or honey is added just before the dish is served so that the grains of wheat don't harden.

According to popular Greek belief, all the other ingredients in the *sperna* play their own symbolic role – the grapes evoke the words of Christ, the sesame seeds represent life and fecundity, and the almonds symbolise the blanched bones of humans when they're dead and of the vanity of life. The pomegranate is also associated with the world of the dead. In mythology, Hades, god of the underworld, sent one as a gift to Persephone, daughter of Demeter, so that she would remain in his kingdom and become his wife.

Rinse the grains of durum wheat. Tip them into a large pan filled with cold salted water. Bring to the boil and cook for 5–10 minutes until the wheat has become soft.

Rinse the cooked wheat in a strainer under cold running water.

Lay a thick dish towel on your work surface, tip the drained wheat onto it and spread out to a thin layer with your fingers. Leave to dry out for 6–8 hours.

Put the wheat into a bowl, and stir in the chopped almonds, walnut pieces, sesame seeds, both types of raisin, the dragees, and pomegranate seeds (keep back a few of each for decoration).

Sprinkle the cinnamon, cardamom, coriander, cumin, and breadcrumbs on top and stir well again.

Arrange the mixture in a shallow dish. Decorate with the reserved almonds, dragees, and pomegranate seeds. Serve cold, handing round the sugar and honey separately.

Medley of

Preparation time:	*1 hour*
Cooking time:	*40 minutes*
Difficulty:	★★★

Serves 4

about 18 sheets	phyllo (filo) pastry
9 oz/250 g	unsalted butter, melted

Filling for the baklava and saragli:

1½ cups/200 g	chopped almonds
1½ cups/200 g	chopped walnuts
4 tsp	grated nutmeg
4 tsp	ground cinnamon

Filling for the petalaki:

¾ cup/100 g	sesame seeds

Filling for the mandilaki:

1 lb/450 g	pine nuts
¾ cup/100 g	dried prunes

For the syrup:

2¼ lb/1 kg	sugar
½	orange
½	lemon
1 stick	cinnamon

If you had to come up with a quick list of Greek dishes known all over the world, it would include the famous moussaka, of course; the classic Greek Salad made with feta, olives, cucumber and tomatoes; *souvlakia*, delicious chunks of lamb cooked on a skewer; not forgetting, of course, a whole range of refreshing *mezze*. This list, nowhere near exhaustive, would not be complete without *baklava* and other sweet pastries.

Extremely popular, these delights use dried fruit and syrup and were first made in the magnificent city of Thessalonika (Salonika) in Macedonia. They have different names depending on the shape of the pastry and the filling, and are usually eaten in the afternoon with friends over a cup of strong Greek coffee, accompanied by a glass of water.

They require patience to make and attention to detail, but these deliciously crunchy little confections epitomize the elegance of Greek cuisine. The sheets of phyllo (filo) are usually rectangular in shape and need careful handling because they are very fragile. They tend to dry out when left uncovered, so cover them with a damp cloth. Made from sifted flour, salt, yeast, water, and sometimes olive oil, phyllo pastry is often still home made. For this recipe, you will need three packs of phyllo, each containing six sheets.

The fillings are a rich source of energy and use dried fruit to great effect. Loved since the days of Ancient Greece, the combination of walnuts, almonds, and prunes make a very happy marriage of flavors and textures. Sotiris Evangelou suggests you try this recipe with some pistachios as well, which grow in abundance on the island of Aegina.

In Greek tradition, the little pastry bundles are arranged in a round shallow aluminum dish known as a *tapsi* before they are baked, taken to the table and served immediately.

Mix the filling ingredients for the baklava and saragli. Butter a phyllo sheet, put another on top and butter, then spread with a quarter of the filling. Fold in the outer edges and form into a roll.

Repeat the previous operation to make a second roll. Butter a fifth sheet, put another on top and butter. Place on top the 2 filled rolls alongside each other, then roll up. Cut the baklava pinwheels into small round slices.

For the saragli: Butter a sheet of phyllo. Place another sheet on top and butter it. Add the remaining filling, top with another butter sheet and roll up tightly around a narrow stick to keep the roll thin. Press between your fingers and carefully remove the stick.

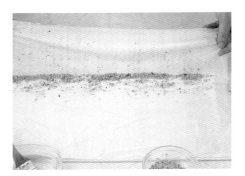

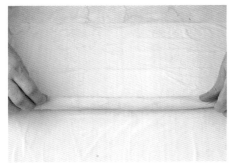

Salonikan Delights

For the petalaki: Butter 1 sheet of phyllo. Scatter over sesame seeds, and fold in half. Butter another sheet of phyllo and fold in half. Lay the 2 sheets on top of each other and roll. Butter a third sheet and roll it around the roll. Cut into sections and form horseshoe shapes.

For the mandilaki: Butter the remaining sheets of phyllo and layer them. Cut into rectangles. Put pine nuts in some, prunes in others, and fold into a pouch shape.

Butter the tapsi dish and arrange the delights as shown. Butter again. Bake in an oven preheated to 350° F/180° C for about 40 minutes. Make a syrup with the ingredients and pour over the delights.

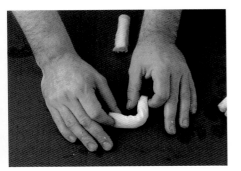

The

George Anastassakis

Panagiotis Delvenakiotis

Sotiris Evangelou

Miltos Karoubas

Nicolaos Katsanis

Stefanos Kovas

Chefs

Aristedes Pasparakis

Nikos Sarandos

Konstantinos and Chrysanthi Stamkopoulos

Anastasios Tolis

Évie Voutsina

Abbreviations:

1 oz = 1 ounce = 28 grams
1 lb = 1 pound = 16 ounces
1 cup = 8 ounces* (see below)
1 cup = 8 fluid ounces = 250 milliliters (liquids)
2 cups = 1 pint (liquids)
1 glass = 4–6 fluid ounces = 125–150 ml (liquids)
1 tbsp = 1 level tablespoon = 15-20 g* (see below) = 15 milliliters (liquids)
1 tsp = 1 level teaspoon = 3-5 g* (see below) = 5 ml (liquids)
1 kg = 1 kilogram = 1000 grams
1 g = 1 gram = 1/1000 kilogram
1 l = 1 liter = 1000 milliliters = approx. 34 fluid ounces
1 ml = 1 milliliter = 1/1000 liter

*The weight of dry ingredients varies significantly depending on the density factor, e.g. 1 cup flour weighs less than 1 cup butter. Quantities in ingredients have been rounded up or down for convenience, where appropriate. Metric conversions may therefore not correspond exactly. It is important to use either American or metric measurements within a recipe.

© for the original edition: Fabien Bellahsen and Daniel Rouche

Concept and production: Fabien Bellahsen, Daniel Rouche
Photos and technical management: Didier Bizos
Editors: Elodie Bonnet, Nathalie Talhouas
Editorial assistant: Fabienne Ripon
Interpreters: Hélène Milakis, Katerina Spyropoulou
With the kind collaboration of: Maria Stephanides, Elga Association
Thanks to:
Andonis Panaytopoulos, President of the Greek Academy of Taste
Nikos Psilakis, Vice-president of the Greek Academy of Taste
Nikos Skoulas, Honorary President of the Greek Academy of Taste, and ex-Minister of Tourism
Yannis Patellis, President of the Greek National Tourist Office
Grecotel and Iston Bay Hotel

Original title: *Délices de Grèce*
ISBN of the original edition: 2-84690-242-9
ISBN of the German edition: 3-8331-2326-5

© 2006 for the English edition:
Tandem Verlag GmbH
KÖNEMANN is a trademark and an imprint of Tandem Verlag GmbH

Translated from the French:
Marilyn Myerscough for First Edition Translations Ltd, Cambridge, UK
Editor: Lin Thomas for First Edition Translations Ltd
Typesetting and project management: First Edition Translations Ltd

Project Coordination: Isabel Weiler

Printed in Germany

ISBN 3-8331-2327-3

10 9 8 7 6 5 4 3 2 1
X IX VIII VII VI V IV III II I